Lowcountry
Born

Ruth P. Saunders

ISBN: 978-1-948604-79-6 (Paperback)

ISBN: 978-1-948604-83-3 (Ebook)

Library of Congress Control Number: 2020910338

Prepared for Publishing by Write|Publish|Sell

Cover Design by Fresh Design

Copyediting & Manuscript Coaching by Lauren Clark

Photography by Gordon Humphries

This collection is dedicated to the memory of my parents.

Table of Contents

Low Country Born

Briars growing by the roadside
Hot sun, some burning sand
Thunderstorms on summer days
Sudden rain cooling thirsty land.

Warm and colorful autumn
Dark cool swamps, brilliant trees
A hint of approaching winter
Felt in a chilling breeze.

Southern winter, short and windswept
Subsides—the birds start to sing
Once again there is renewal of life
With the return of a Low Country Spring.

This is my beloved birthplace
Land of moods stormy and mild
A land generous, healing, forgiving
I'm glad I'm a Low Country Child!

By my mother, Ruth [J.] Saunders (1926-2013),
from *Low Country Children*, 1986

Introduction

This lighthearted collection of stories and essays describes my growing up in rural, Lowcountry South Carolina and my continued evolution beyond those early years. The writing began sporadically some years ago, became more frequent after Momma died in 2013, and grew more focused after Daddy died in 2018. The writing process has helped me celebrate and honor the lives of my parents, appreciate how early experiences shaped me as a person, and value the many past and present positives in my life.

I wrote this collection with family and friends in mind as well as to entertain others. For family and friends, it is intended to collect and preserve memories, and for all readers, I hope it triggers positive recollections from the past. Much of the joy in putting this collection together was working with my sister and brother to reconstruct details and to reminisce about the many delightful memories we share. Reviewing the past had the unexpected benefit of increasing enjoyment of the present and enabling me to cope with losing Momma and Daddy.

Each of the first four sections begins with an essay followed by several stories. Section I, "Places of Origin," describes the physical settings of my childhood and memories connected to those places. I begin here because the stories that follow can be more fully appreciated in context, and because where I was "born and bred" is a part of who I am. Sections II through IV follow in more-or-less chronological order, each with an essay and series of story-memories. Section II, "Childhood Imaginings," describes mostly childhood recollections, Section III, "Driven to Distraction," spans adolescent experiences and beyond, and Section IV, "Letting Go," celebrates my parents and their mothers. Section

V, "Triple Star System," is an essay tribute to my siblings, and Section VI, "Family Recipes," contains the recipes mentioned within the stories of this collection and is a concrete way of preserving and passing on family memories.

I

Places of Origin

> We are surrounded by places. We walk over and through them. We
> live in places, relate to others in them, die in them. Nothing we do
> is unplaced. How could it be otherwise? How could we fail to rec-
> ognize this primal fact?
>
> — Edward S. Casey,
> *The Fate of Place: A Philosophical History*

The rural Lowcountry of South Carolina defines how the world should be to me: level terrain; black, rich dirt; a cacophony of green grasses, flowers, garden plants, bushes, vines, and trees; and abundant water in creeks, swamps, and rivers that lead to the Atlantic Ocean. Living creatures occupy every niche; fascinating objects, from fossils in rocks to sand dollars on the beach, are in plain view, waiting for a child to discover them.

"Places of Origin" describes formative places in my life, in and around my home in rural Colleton County. As a Low Country Child, I spent a lot of time outdoors, so this is where we begin—with the wetlands that permeate the Low-country, the immediate areas surrounding the home in which I grew up, the yard around the house, and then, finally, inside my childhood home. The final piece is not about where I lived, but a place I visited—Edisto Beach—a central place in my heart that feels like home and anchors me to South Carolina.

Wildness and Wet

What would the world be, once bereft
Of wet and of wildness? Let them be left,
O let them be left, wildness and wet;
Long live the weeds and the wilderness yet.

— Gerard Manley Hopkins, Inversnaid

Swamps and marshes were part of my life growing up, the natural order of things. I see them as dark gems embedded throughout the Low-country. They stimulated my childhood curiosity and imagination and helped me develop a deep respect for mother nature and her sometimes enigmatic ways of doing her job. In these eclectic and diverse habitats, everything seems to fit in, and even supposed unseemly organisms have important roles. In this way, they invite acceptance and the realization that just because something is not understood, doesn't mean it is not important. Lowcountry swamps and marshes frame the place where I belong and are part of my home.

Many find the wooded, shadowy swamps and murky, grassy marshes uninviting, as though something sinister, possibly evil, lies below. But I have always been drawn to their wetness, wildness, and mystery. It does not summon me to wade in the swamp or marsh, where the unknown resides. Instead, it calls to observation, imagination, and reflection.

Swamps near my home community of Stokes are populated with cypress, gum, oak, and maple trees. They rise from black water, some at peculiar angles, amid a tangle of water-loving shrubs, bushes, and vines. Fallen branches and twigs are strewn about in water and on patches of land. Sunlight diffuses through the thick canopy above, creating large dark shadows interspersed with sudden splashes of light. At first sight, it appears that chaos abounds, but observation reveals a natural order.

These seemingly inert bodies of water are teaming with life and activity. Stand silently on the edge of a swamp or marsh and listen to the pops, cracks, and cries. The air may be pierced with the sudden flapping of wings with an alarm call as you catch a glimpse of a departing bird. You may hear an abrupt gurgle and see a gentle disturbance before you realize you just witnessed a submerging turtle. Life is subtle here, for the most part, but it permeates the swamp.

Wetlands are essential for our planet. They retard erosion, stabilize shorelines, act as a reservoir, and with the help of resident plants and microorganisms, trap pollutants, remove excess nutrients, and purify water. It is wonderful that mud and microbes, so seemingly dark and dirty, are quietly cleaning up. They are the most biologically diverse of all ecosystems, providing breeding grounds and homes for a wide range of plants and animals. Swamps may be life at its best.

Lowcountry swamps and coastal marshes form alongside slow-moving rivers and creeks. One of my earliest memories is Doctor's Creek, which runs through the family property. Most of the time it was tucked inconspicuously into the woods; a small, sluggish body of water the color of strong iced tea. But when heavy rain produced flooding, the creek escaped its boundaries, seeped into the woods and flowed several feet deep across Ruffin Road, rather than under it through a culvert. I wanted to wade and swim in the newly formed pool, but floodwaters can be unsafe, and we were not allowed to play in them. Prepared farmers such as my father placed canals around low fields to drain excess water and prevent crop damage from occasional floods.

The Colleton County landmass is a tapestry of creeks, rivers, and wetlands, with the Combahee and Edisto Rivers forming its western and eastern borders. Doctor's Creek intertwines with Penny and Ireland Creeks and Jones and Ivanhoe Swamps. These braided bodies of water feed into the Great Swamp Sanctuary in Walterboro and give rise to the Ashepoo River.

The Ashepoo, along with its sisters Combahee and Edisto, derive their names from Cusabo Native American subtribes and flow into Saint Helena

Sound, finally reaching the Atlantic Ocean at Edisto Beach. Colleton County doesn't have shoreline on the Atlantic Ocean, but it is, by these rivers, connected to the sea. It is no wonder that I have always felt linked to the ocean.

Braided bodies of water are also common in the coastal marshes and fascinate me as places of beauty, complexity, and mystery. As a child, with a strong sense of home as a specific place, I wondered how the creatures living within them kept from becoming confused and lost. As an adult, I marvel that streams could be so interrelated as part of one thing yet keep their own identities. We could learn a lot from them, if only we are patient enough to listen.

The paths of the channels shift, as though each day the water plans the best route to achieve its goal of becoming part of the Atlantic. When I rode my bicycle on creek overpasses on the rural roads as a child, I would often stop and gaze at the dark liquid flowing by, wandering slowly but surely to the sea. I felt connected to the creek, to the ocean, and to the planet. I witnessed part of the global dance of water moving above, on, and under the earth.

Swamps and marshes are on the edges, where land meets water and boundaries are blurred. They abide by a different set of rules. Through the ebb and flow of floods and tides, dramatic change is routine. Trees that usually grow on land like you and I, can drown, but trees in swamps flourish with their roots underwater. Cypress trees are resilient and grow in many habitats including parking lots; they thrive in swamps by producing "cypress knees," peculiar, 1- to 3-foot tall, cone-shaped root extensions. I enjoyed visiting the publicly accessible cypress swamps, such as Magnolia Gardens in Moncks Corner, and found cypress knees fascinating. But public swamps do not evoke the sense of mystery and awe inspired by the remote swamps that formed the backdrop for my childhood home.

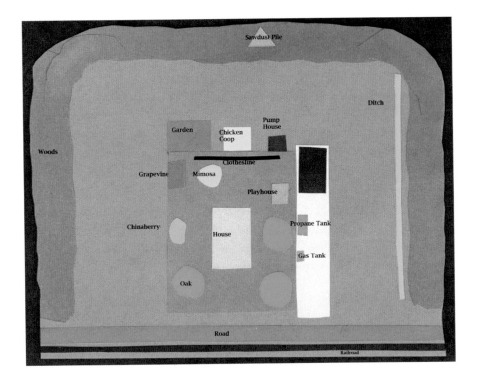

Around My Childhood Home

Our family home was the center of my childhood universe. Modest by today's standards, it was set in the rural Lowcountry South Carolina community of Stokes. The house, yard, and its surroundings shaped my experiences growing up, are woven into the fabric of my being, and are a central character in this collection.

I was an active child and spent much time outside. The front yard was bordered by a road and a railroad track, and the back yard and both side yards were enclosed by fields, which were surrounded by a pine forest. I spent as much time playing in the outer areas bordering the house, the railroad track, fields, and forest as I did in the yard and house. This is a brief memory-tour of the place that helped shape who I am.

Route 3

We lived on a farm-to-market road that bounded the front yard. Traffic moved at a minimum of 55 miles per hour on this highway, so we were warned to stay away from it and crossing it required adult supervision. Early on the address was Route 3, but in the early-to-mid 1980s the highway was renamed Ruffin Road, and the house was given a street number for 911 services identification.

A freight train track ran parallel to the road in front of the house, and trains passed regularly when we were growing up. I raced the train on my bicycle as it passed in front of our house. I heard it coming and stationed myself at a starting point on one edge of the yard for a moving start. I had marked a segment of the front yard in which I tried to keep up with it, but it always outraced me. Losing the race didn't matter, though – it was thrilling to try. I imagine the conductor found this repeated ritual amusing. Other times my siblings and I waved at the man standing on the caboose at the end of the train hoping he would toot the whistle at us. When he did, we exploded with delight at being acknowledged. My sister, brother, and I spent time on the tracks with adult supervision, collecting rocks, flattening nickels, and picking wild blackberries. We were fascinated by the flattened coins. Part of the attraction was the fear that a well-placed coin would derail the train.

Over the years the rail was operated by ACL (Atlantic Coast Line), SCL (Seaboard Coast Line), and CSX (Chessie Seaboard Merger). When I was young, I was puzzled by the rail cars labeled with these letters, intermingled with graffiti. I didn't understand the acronyms or the complex history of railroad company mergers. When I was about 10, the railroad company built a branch line through the field on the left side of the house, to service the coal-powered Canadys Power Station. The Canadys Station has since been decommissioned and trains no longer run.

The Fields

Our house and yard were bordered by fields on the back and sides, spanning about 17 acres. Daddy planted soybeans or corn during the warm growing season and winter wheat during the cool growing season, but soybeans were the chief crop. In the spring, after planting, I ran barefooted in the furrows of newly planted soybeans and felt the soil warm on top, cool and moist underneath as my feet sank into it. Running up and down the rows was an expression of the sheer joy of my childhood.

Daddy spot checked for sprouting soybeans shortly after sowing the seeds and soon the pale green seedlings rose through the ground. By late summer the deep green soybean bushes towered over me. I looked closely to see the small flowers that would become "baby pods" – they were covered in a fine plant fuzz and contained the developing soybeans. Supported by rain and sun, the soybeans grew within their pod "nurseries."

By Thanksgiving, the entire plant and its fruit had turned a dry golden-brown and produced full-sized beans inside visible clusters of pods, ready for gathering. Daddy guided the combine through the field harvesting the treasures. It was unpleasant and dusty work on an open harvester—today's farmers sit in enclosed, air-conditioned cabins for protection. Daddy never seemed to mind, but over the years the soybean dust damaged his breathing.

Farmers are at the mercy of mother nature, but most years Daddy's crops produced well. I appreciated the plants for their contribution to our livelihood – soybeans paid my way through college. But there were less tangible and more enduring benefits. I watched a small seed grow into a large complex plant for the purpose of creating more seeds in an endless cycle and wondered if the purpose of life were simply to perpetuate itself.

Tadpole Dreams

When it rained, a common occurrence, water accumulated in the flat field, especially at the edges where it drowned growing seedlings. Daddy dug a drainage canal on the far edge of the field that spared the plants. It was fondly known as the "big ditch" and was a great place to play. My sister, brother, and I made boats from wood and paper and attempted to sail them and experimented with building water wheels there, though it's difficult to imagine how that worked since the terrain was flat.

The ditch reached through the rich topsoil into clay that I scooped out and shaped into small objects. I air dried the small sculptures made from this special clay to harden them into semi-permanent pieces. I was especially proud of an elephant figurine. My sister was so intrigued by the miniature pachyderm she tested its durability by dropping it to the floor. It was an early lesson about the impermanence of human-made things.

The clear, still water in the canal created the ideal habitat for toads at all stages of their life cycle. The transformation from eggs to tadpoles and then toads was astounding and otherworldly to me. I spent many hours watching and learning. This was the place where tadpoles dreamed of becoming toads and where I dreamed of witnessing the transformation.

I visited the ditch every day to check the water until I saw the eggs—black dots dispersed evenly throughout thin ropes of gooey stuff. Over the days the dark dots would grow tiny tails and break through the egg casing, becoming tadpoles. For hours I watched them wriggle about, stop and nibble on the sandy bottom or an underwater leaf.

Eventually the growing tadpoles sprouted four little legs. The legs grew while the tail shrunk over time. And then one day the tadpoles were gone, having taken to land as the toads they were destined to be. I never saw a tadpole make the crucial transition at the water's edge and hop away from its aquatic birthplace. No matter how hard I tried, I was never at the ditch at the right moment to see baby amphibians emerge. This challenge needed a scientific approach, and I knew from my science books that observation was the main tool of a scientist.

I reasoned the best way to observe the transition was to bring the tadpoles into my bedroom in a shallow pan with water and sand from the ditch. Under my watchful eye they would complete their metamorphosis. This investigative plan was a stroke of genius, and it would save me hours of observing at the ditch with uncertain outcomes.

Sadly, this experiment was repeated unsuccessfully several times. Who knows how many tadpoles met their demise in my bedroom. I tried everything my 8-year-old scientific brain could muster: putting them in different containers; using soil, water and plants from different places in the ditch; and feeding them guppy food as a last resort. Nothing worked. The loss of the little creatures was a tragedy to me, and I felt responsible for their untimely deaths. I have since learned that as few as two tadpoles from a batch of hundreds of eggs make it to the hatching stage and survive to reproduce as toads before being eaten. Perhaps my short-lived childhood "experiments" didn't damage the amphibian population too much.

My grand bedroom-as-laboratory endeavor ended with a simple but persuasive argument from my mother. She explained the tadpoles and their mother missed each other, so I should let them stay in the ditch. It didn't matter that I had never seen a momma toad anxiously waiting near the water, attending eggs or tadpoles. Momma's argument made sense to me. Scientific discovery would have to wait.

The Woods

A forest, populated by tall pine trees, surrounded the fields; we called it *the woods*. In the spring and fall I spent hours walking around the edges, often venturing inside. It was a special place where I stood among tall pines as they whispered in the breeze. This reassured me at a deep level. They seemed wise but I didn't understand the whispered message until later: what one can learn by being still and listening.

I loved the upturned trees that had fallen on their sides, exposing their underground root bases. Interesting mosses, mushrooms, and lichens grew on and around them. I sensed this was a small world within a world, populated by unusual living things. Later in life I learned mosses are simple plants reproducing without flowers or seeds, tree mushrooms are bracket fungi reproducing by spores, and lichens are algae and fungi living together. I am fascinated by the diversity of living arrangements in nature that take advantage of every available niche and am delighted moss grows plentifully in my Columbia yard today.

My siblings and I built huts in the woods, especially when first cousins were visiting to help with the work. We gathered fallen pine limbs and propped them against a pine tree, forming half a teepee. The limbs were covered with gathered clean pine straw. We pretended we lived there. We also tried to build traps for bunnies, but we were not very good at it, so all the bunnies were quite safe. We spent hours living in the woods, the perfect childhood playground.

Deciduous trees, mostly dogwoods and maples, grew on the edges of the pine forest. In the spring Maples produced winged red seed pairs, turning the tree scarlet. I watched the colors change from spring red to summer green and to yellow and red in fall. My rhythm for the passage of time was set by watching the trees change. I felt sad about the loss of leaves and the leafless branches during the winter season but learned about hope and renewal from the cycles of nature. No matter how bare the trees and how cold and dark the days, spring always returns.

I loved to climb these trees and spent hours viewing the rural scenery from them. It was a good way to spend time alone. I believed no one could find me when I was in one of my hide-a-way trees. But when I once commented, "I bet you didn't know where I was this afternoon," my mother set me straight. She knew exactly where I was: in my secret dogwood tree at the edge of the field! My small collie dog followed me everywhere and Momma explained, "When you are up a tree, Prince is curled up at the bottom. I always know where you are." And that was probably just as well.

Ghost of Stokes

A lone, mysterious sawdust pile was tucked away in the woods behind the house; my brother, sister, and I played on it. It was attractive because adults admonished us to stay away, and we believed it was dangerous. At any moment a hole might open and swallow a person who would never be seen again, or hidden flames smoldering for years might suddenly burst forth. Our shared fantasies made playing on the sawdust pile exciting and fun.

Daddy explained our secret sawdust pile was a remnant of a large sawmill during the heyday of Stokes, when "Stokes was really Stokes." When he was around 5 years old, Stokes was a lumber town centered around Patilla's Sawmill, which had its own logging railroad extending into the woods.

Daddy's family operated two businesses, a turpentine still and a cotton gin. Mr. Maxey was the postmaster and depot man. The Maxeys were good friends with Daddy's family. I heard the stories about the Stokes' golden days from Daddy, but it was far removed from the community I knew as a child. I never had any doubts, though. The sawdust pile ghost was a testament to Stokes' history, as well as my own.

The Yard of
My Childhood Home

The yard of my childhood home was a wonderful playground. In hot weather, we put on our bathing suits and frolicked around a water sprinkler. As temperatures dropped around dusk, lightning bugs flashed. At least that's what we called them; most people refer to them as fireflies. The cool, silent lights blinking low to the ground in the darkening evening seemed magical. The bugs paid no attention to us and were easy to catch as they were tending to the more pressing matter of propagating their species. Daddy showed us how to catch and safely release them. He demonstrated slowly walking up to a flashing insect, carefully cupping hands around it, peeking at the flashes inside your closed hands, and then letting it go. It was the perfect end to a summer day.

Our yard held many attractions—a treehouse, grapevine, clothesline, playhouse, vegetable garden, chickenyard, barn, and two gas tanks. This rural amusement park was a magnet for children and we often played there with cousins and friends.

Penthouse

Several live oaks, a Chinaberry, and a crepe myrtle, as well as mimosa, mulberry, apple and pear trees thrived in our yard. I loved trees and wanted a treehouse, preferably a small multi-room house somehow perched in a tree. I didn't think through the engineering and construction skills required for this feat. Never mind that, though, because Daddy had self-attained skills in both areas. He was also a very practical man with a finite amount of time and energy.

The treehouse I got was a nice platform in the Chinaberry, one of my favorite trees, with its small, fragrant, lavender flowers in the spring and deep green leaves in the summer. It was in the side yard with a view of the field and the woods—the perfect place for a treehouse.

I spent hours in my penthouse, a much more comfortable place for singing, daydreaming, and sightseeing than perched on a branch in a tree. I sometimes imagined I was a wild cat, at home and quite comfortable with my body draped on a tree branch. But I was not of the feline persuasion and liked having the sturdy platform for support. I took my lofty abode for granted at the time. But in the years since, when I return to that happy place in my mind, I thank my father.

Giant Green Cake

There were many cookouts, often for birthday celebrations, as my sister and my best friend were born in the spring. I enjoyed smelling the aromas of grilled hot dogs and hamburgers as much as eating them. I remember the gathering of children, the excitement of games such as "hide-and-seek," "red rover," and "stoplight," and the anticipation of opening gifts. The boisterous crowd could also play on the swing set, climb on the pumphouse, or "ride" the propane tank "horse." The swing had flat, hard seats that are no longer available in the current safety-conscious world. I used to swing as high as I could and was thrilled to imagine that I could wrap all the way around the top bars if I wanted to, especially if I could convince a sibling, friend, or cousin to give me a push. But the main event was cake and ice cream.

Momma baked a special birthday treat, known as the "giant green cake." She had a baking pan which resembled a sheet cakepan, but with thicker walls and a warp on the bottom resulting in a uniquely shaped cake. Two cake mixes filled the pan. She iced it with "butter icing," made from margarine, confectioner's sugar, and vanilla flavoring. The frosting was always tinted light green and adorned with premade "Happy Birthday" decorations available in the local grocery store.

These confections did not reflect high-end cake decorating, but they did convey Momma's love and attention; they were also tasty, and everyone loved to eat them. My sister, brother and I still talk about the giant green cakes. When we cleaned out our parent's home after Daddy passed away, I was delighted to find the special baking pan amid dusty pots and pans

after being lost for years before Momma died. I plan to introduce the newest generation, our parent's great grands, to the "giant green cake." I can't imagine a childhood without it.

The Wild West

The chicken yard enclosure with egg-laying hens was tucked between the back yard and field. I played there, pretending chickens were cows, and I was a cowboy herding them. Chickens were not cooperative herding stock, but it was fun seeing their shiny, brown, feathery backs and bobbing heads as they scampered ahead of me. Momma didn't stop me, though in retrospect this surely affected egg production. We produced eggs for home consumption; maybe the feathered ladies laid plenty even though they were chased around the chickenyard or maybe their increased fitness improved egg production. In later years we kept a small number of beef cattle, but by then I was too old to play cowboy. Plus, the cattle were intimidating and big compared to chickens.

We played "rodeo" on the propane gas tank by pretending it was a bucking bronco or crazed bull. It was a large silver horizontal cylinder tank that supplied gas for heating and cooking in the house. I was always afraid it would explode, which made for an exhilarating ride on a stationary object. A rural upbringing fosters a vivid imagination. There was also a fuel pump to supply gasoline for the farm and family vehicles, but it held little interest until we became old enough to drive a car. Dreams of automobiles replaced childhood fantasy horses and cattle by the time of adolescence for my friends, but I did not give up childhood as quickly.

For Adults Only

Momma dried clothes for a family of five on a clothesline in the backyard which meant she spent a lot of time there. We usually played in the yard, but when I was tall enough, I sometimes helped hang out the clothes. I can still smell the fresh, clean laundry after being air-dried in the sunshine and feel the slightly coarse but pleasant texture of the fabric on my skin, even though it has been years since I've had that pleasure.

I liked to watch the laundry flap in the breeze as it hung on the clothesline, especially the sheets. It could be hypnotic, like watching waves on the ocean. My dog Prince enjoyed the flapping sheets more directly—by shredding them with his teeth. Momma discouraged this with the aid of a broom but was never successful. In the wintertime the clothes froze on the line occasionally, hanging and flapping stiffly in the wind, as though they were occupied by two-dimensional beings trying to escape.

The garden was near the clothesline and another place to find Momma working. We were privileged to eat fresh vegetables and fruits during the long Lowcountry growing season. I looked forward to strawberries in spring from the garden and ate them straight from the plant, dirt and all. Little compared to eating a fresh strawberry warmed by the sun. I sometimes picked enough to make pies or jam by reciting "keep two, eat one." Okra picked, whisked to the frying pan, and eaten within an hour was a special pleasure that cannot be replicated by food bought in a grocery store or served in a restaurant. The garden was for serious food but sometimes a pack of children, usually siblings and cousins, would scavenge produce for pretend cooking. Once my sister and a first cousin picked every green tomato in the garden for a play project. Momma was not pleased about this.

Not far from the garden and clothesline was the pumphouse, which was Daddy's domain. It protected the electric pump which drew water from the well on the property, a common practice in rural areas then and now. Daddy switched on a single lightbulb in the small building to prevent freezes in cold weather and, during power outages, fretted over losing the pump's prime, which enabled it to draw water. Momma and Daddy told me about how the shallow well we had when I was born delivered debris along with water. I remember when the deep well was drilled, tapping into an underground aquafer. I tried to imagine the underground river, but it was difficult. I hoped it flowed through underground rocks rather than clay, because that seemed a lot cleaner. We weren't supposed to climb onto the pumphouse but did so anyway, because it provided a slightly elevated view. But we lost interest in pumphouse perching when Momma started feeding the cats on top of it to keep the dogs from eating their food.

Barn Cats

Tractors, plows, and other farm equipment as well as discarded items such as the old furniture, pumps, and spent motor oil were kept in the barn or under its sheds. It was a great place to explore. The surplus water pump was a curious device with whirly-wheels and various moveable gadgets on top of a small cylindrical tank. It made an intriguing toy for my sister and me—we treated it as a communication device for conversing with aliens in outer space. Momma must have gotten a kick out of seeing her two little girls turning wheels and gadgets and talking to the pump. We spent most of the time contacting Tinker-Tinker, a cat living on Mars. These conversations were one-sided, but we enjoyed them anyway and spent hours making alien contact with our advanced communication technology.

It was also a great place for earthly cats, and ours were prolific producers of kittens. My sister, brother, and I learned early in life that not all cats who have kittens make good mothers. There was one cat who regularly became "with kitten" and had not a clue what to do with the offspring after birth. She moved them to unsafe places such as the bottom of a ditch shortly before a rainstorm. We tried to find them before it was too late, but there really wasn't much we could do. As a kitten she had survived a dunk in the open drum of discarded motor oil under the barn. She was quickly retrieved after being thrown in by one of my brother's friends; we cleaned her as best we could, but she was saturated with oil. She grew up to have luxurious fur but was never an ordinary cat after the "baptism."

My first lesson on the "birds and the bees" was prompted by my questions about where kittens come from. Momma explained that the daddy cat gave the momma cat a seed and the kittens grew from that. She did not describe *how* he gave her the seed, but I observed that myself. I was stunned a few years later when I learned that that same process applies to people.

Cats often found hiding places in the barn to give birth. They were secretive about the birthing process, which made it difficult to witness. This was something I wanted to see because I was curious, and I imagined myself as a stealthy cat tracker. On one lucky day, I followed a momma-to-be-cat's indirect path to the spot she had selected in the barn, carefully maintaining an unobtrusive distance. I waited until she had checked out the area and became quiet, out of sight in a hidden box inside the barn. After waiting a long time to be sure it had started, I quietly approached.

Seeing the birth of five tiny kittens was no big deal because I had expected babies to come out of the momma cat. But I was amazed at what took place next. She spent hours licking the naked babies to remove the remnants of the birthing process—she carefully cleaned each kitten as though it were the only one. The task seemed tedious and unpleasant to me, but she did not hurry. I reasoned in my 10-year-old mind that the momma cat really loved her babies. Reflecting on it now, momma cat's behavior was driven more by instinct than love. But biologically speaking, perhaps they are the same thing. Love may be more about what you do than what you feel.

The Playhouse

The playhouse, a small outbuilding, stood in the side yard near the barn. Daddy hauled this small one-room building into the backyard for me, my sister, and my brother. It had a kitchen containing a toy stove with no actual heat, play dishes, and real dishes from the house. We made mud pies in the playhouse and pretended the seed pods on the Mimosa tree were beans and "cooked" them. We had another recipe for making a mush out of acorns and Chinaberry Tree berries. The dish was bitter which is just as well because Chinaberry berries are toxic to humans.

The playhouse kitchen is where I discovered my love of "stirring things up," at least if they were fixings in a bowl. I transformed dirt and water pies into something special by adding eggs from the chickenyard to the mixture. I experimented with differing amounts of water, dirt, and eggs to get the most luxurious textures in my mud pies. The final product was always dark, far more so than chocolate, because we used dirt from the edge of Daddy's field. Low-country dirt is black—rich, fertile, and one of the best substances on the planet, in my opinion.

A few years later I moved my mixing operations indoors and started using edible ingredients to make cakes, cookies, and candies. With the help of experts including my mother, grandmothers, aunts, and mother of my best friend, I learned how to mix batter to the proper texture prior to baking. I still enjoy stirring sauce, icing, or batter, as well as making a mess in the kitchen. But mixing mud pies with eggs will always occupy a special place in my heart as my first recipe.

There was one misadventure in the playhouse. Momma was not at home and the caretaker was in the house. My preschool-aged brother and first cousin entertained themselves by jumping out of the playhouse window, which was dangerous enough. But before jumping they threw glass dishes from the windows. My brother landed on a broken dish and cut a deep gash in his foot which bleed profusely. After initial chaos, he was rushed to the emergency room for stitches. Fortunately, the wound healed completely, and it left a scar that he could display as a badge of childhood honor.

Near the playhouse we had a basketball goal where Daddy shot baskets with my sister, brother, and I. We played individual scoring games such as our version of "21," to see who would be the first to accumulate 21 points. Daddy held the developmental advantage in the early years; one of us three children often left in tears or frustration. That changed when I grew larger, became more skilled, and started beating Daddy. I don't believe he ever stormed away from the game, but he clearly preferred winning. Or maybe he resisted his children's growing up and catching up with parents.

*   *   *

The yard and all of its special places feel as real in my memory now as they did when I daydreamed in the treehouse, enjoyed the Giant Green Cake, herded chicken-cows, witnessed mother-cat-love, and played in and around the play-house. The structures of this safe, fascinating, and fun place shaped the fundamental architecture of my brain. It is comforting and never far away.

Inside My Childhood Home

As much as I enjoyed the outdoors with its adventures, the indoors of my childhood home was always the safe haven, a retreat from the world, and a rich source of memories. This is a memory-tour inside of the home that raised me.

Entryway

A short concrete sidewalk originating mid-yard led to brick steps and onto the open front porch with modest white columns made of wood. The entrance to the house also served as the gateway to lessons learned while growing up. I once crawled across the porch and lapped up lead-based paint from the freshly coated columns. Momma took me to the doctor because lead is toxic and harms mental and physical development in young children, but no one discerned any ill effects. In later years I mused about having my life as a genius abruptly curtailed by a snack of white paint before I learned to walk, though I wonder if a child prodigy would have ingested wet pigment. In my defense, the paint probably looked like melted ice cream.

When a little older, I rode a tricycle off the edge of the porch into a bush which fortunately cushioned the fall. It was frightening and my screams brought Momma to investigate and extract me and my tricycle from the scratchy branches. I learned an important lesson about the force of gravity that day, or at least I never fell from the edge of the porch again.

I learned to roller-skate on the sidewalk, a short piece of flat concrete ideal for learning. Skating longer distances required a visit to the sidewalk around the block at Grandmother Tulls' house in the town of Walterboro. My skates were metal, fit over my shoes, and opened and closed with a key. Every outing was an adventure because the skates fell apart if I didn't stop every few minutes to tighten them. Even though I was dumped on concrete regularly, I loved it.

When I was older still, my best friend and I sat on the front porch in rocking chairs. We rocked and talked but, because of the boards in the wooden floor, the chairs "walked," so we periodically repositioned them to avoid falling from the side of the porch. Rock, talk, and shift the day away. I can still feel the give of the squeaky boards, but more importantly I feel the friendship sustaining me through childhood and beyond.

Center of Enchantment

The front door opened into the living room, the center of family entertainment. Daddy told my sister, brother, and me stories as we gathered around him in his chair. He had a good singing voice, good enough to perform solos in church, and he sang silly songs to us. One was "Hole in the bottom of the sea," a cumulative song like "The 12 days of Christmas." It starts, *There's a hole in the bottom of the sea, there's a hole in the bottom of the sea, there's a hole, there's a hole, there's a hole in the bottom of the sea.* With each repetition Daddy added an object: log in the hole, knot on the log, frog on the knot, and so on. We delighted in this song, and he invented more and more accumulating objects.

Another favorite was "Mairzy Doats," a novelty song written and composed in 1943 by Milton Drake, Al Hoffman, and Jerry Livingston and became a hit with the Merry Macs' 1944 recording (https://en.wikipedia.org/wiki/Mairzy_Doats). The words in part are:

> *Mairzy doats and dozy doats and liddle lamzy divey*
> *A kiddley divey too, wouldn't you?*
> *Now if the words seem queer and funny to your ear, a little bit jumbled and jivey*
> *Like mares eat oats and does eat oats and little lambs eat ivy.*

Daddy worked long hours during the farming season but fortunately had a down season during cooler weather. During these times his silly side countered his intense "workaholic" side.

From his living room chair Daddy also monitored multiple college games on TV and radio during football season. Before technology made it simple to do it, he sat in front of a TV and placed one radio close to each ear, each broadcasting a different game. His interest in football ran deep—he played in high school and as a semi-professional for a time after that. Later in life he was inducted into the Colleton High Football Hall of Fame. I remember my puzzlement at the first game he took me to see at Walterboro High School. I asked Daddy why, if the players wanted to cross the goal line carrying the ball, everyone kept running together in clumps. It was some time before the game's subtleties, including the challenges of dealing with the opposing team's defense, became clearer to me.

The living room was also the place of honor for the Christmas tree, the core symbol of magic during the holidays. Getting a local cedar tree and decorating it was a family tradition. Finding the perfect tree was easy for a brief time when we were little, because we used the same live tree each year. We found it on our wooded property, dug it up, potted it, brought it to its place of honor in the living room, and decorated it. We watered it over the holidays and then planted it back in the yard shortly after Christmas day. We dug it up the next year and repeated the process for several years until the tree grew too big to move indoors. It is still growing today, decades later, and is quite large. In the past two years, I have revived this tradition by keeping a potted dwarf Spruce in my Columbia yard and bringing it in over the holidays to decorate.

No matter how haphazardly the tree was decorated by enthusiastic children with glass ornaments, tinsel, and a tangle of lights, it assumed an enchanted state when illuminated. Accumulated gifts went under the tree, becoming part of the charm, and Santa Claus added gifts on Christmas Eve after we were in bed. Nothing else compares with the ecstasy of the first sighting of the tree and gifts on Christmas morning. Opening presents was wild, chaotic fun. This ritual might seem to instill a materialistic view of Christmas, but its pervasive feel was one of joy for giving, gratitude for receiving, and looking forward to the promise of the future.

Fascinating Furnishings

A mainstay piece of furniture in the living room was a long, black sofa. It was not particularly attractive but was durable and could hold a lot of people. It survived treatment as a trampoline by small children and, when we were older, seated nervous couples on dates. That sofa served us well and lives in my memory as a character playing an important supporting role in my life.

The dining room was connected to the living room and held a gas heater and an oak dining table with matching chairs. The dining room table came with the house when Momma and Daddy bought it and had ornate legs and insets around the sides, as well as an indented, narrow bottom platform for stability. We ate in the dining room on Sundays and when there were larger gatherings for birthdays and holiday celebrations.

This table was the perfect floor-level jungle gym for small children. My siblings and I played under and ran around it, occasionally getting a nasty bruise or black eye from running into one of the table's corners. We turned the chairs on their sides and covered them with sheets and towels to create hiding places and "rooms," a favorite activity in inclement weather. My sister later raised her two girls in our childhood home, and they showed the table years of additional adventures. Today I am fortunate to have this set in the dining room of my Columbia home after having it professionally stabilized and refinished about 10 years ago. I was told at the time the table and chairs would not survive another generation of children playing under it.

Another curious piece of furniture was a wooden chair with carved lions' heads at the ends of its arms. The lions' mouths were open revealing fangs; their ears were laid back in a snarling roar. I never trusted this chair because the carvings were frightening and seemed real. I wondered if it came alive at night and moved about the house. When I checked, it was always in the same place in the morning, but maybe it had a good memory.

The washing machine "lived" on the back porch. We did not have a clothes dryer because there was a clothesline in the backyard. Momma washed clothes with a ringer washing machine when I was small, but I can barely remember this. I clearly remember the later washing machine: it walked across the back porch during its spin cycle. We took turns leaning heavily on its top to hold it steady. It must have been the combination of the machine's spinning and a slightly sloping floor that produced this effect. With an active family of five, Momma washed clothes continually; the walking machine was almost a member of the family.

Nighttime Spooks

When we were small, my sister and I shared a bedroom and, for a time, a bed. She was easily frightened, a source of entertainment for me. When we were on our backs in bed, she believed me if I lifted my toes up under the sheets and told her little ghosts were at the bottom of the bed and became terrified. She complained about hearing scary "breathing noises in the closet" at night --the family assumed she had an active imagination, which she did, but her hearing was better. Our parents discovered our dog, Samantha, slept under the house below the bedroom closet, and my sister heard the dog snoring. My sister's sensory sensitivity was exquisite. If she announced, "The house shook last night," the news story of the day would be about the overnight earthquake tremor. She trembled in bed, wide awake, while the rest of us slept through it, unaware.

Premature Professor

In one of the back bedrooms Momma hung a large blackboard low on the wall. It was a clever strategy to reduce the amount of writing practice and artwork on the walls. It was also great fun, at least for me. I somehow convinced my younger sister and brother to play school on repeated occasions—I was the teacher and they were the students. I don't remember what I "taught" them, probably whatever I did in school that day.

All three of us eventually worked in educational settings. My sister and I became teachers, and our brother became a school district financial officer. Perhaps I didn't damage them too badly in those early "school days."

The Chefs

The kitchen was an activity center for the family—we spent a lot of time there. There was a breakfast nook where we ate many family meals. This was the informal gathering place for adults who came to visit. Momma loved to sit, drink coffee, and talk with visiting friends and relatives there.

Momma did the day-to-day cooking when we were growing up. Her fried chicken was the best I've ever tasted; it has been years since I've had that privilege because when her three offspring left home, she put down the meat fork and declared, "I'm not frying any more chicken." She stuck to it, and I don't blame her after all those years of braving the hot grease required to make good chicken.

My mother juggled meal preparation and work by developing a weekly meal routine featuring the "menu du jour;" Friday nights were spaghetti nights. Momma devised her own spaghetti sauce recipe, made of ingredients she always had on hand: ground beef and ketchup cooked together and served with a generous topping of grated parmesan cheese. It was easy, fast, and tasty. My best friend would often eat with us.

Once the phone rang while my friend was holding a full plate of spaghetti and sauce in her right hand. With her left hand she answered Daddy's business phone with calm professionalism, "Saunders Fertilizer," and took a message, while she dumped the loaded plate on the floor with no change in demeanor or tone. I've never had that level of aplomb. This memory has provided the family, including my friend, amusement over the years.

Daddy wasn't a regular fixture in the kitchen but on occasions he cooked one of his specialties: omelets or potato chips. The omelets, for breakfast or supper, were made with eggs and cheese plus other ingredients on hand. I didn't care for eggs, so I didn't eat omelets. But I was very interested in the process of making them, and it was a production. He was particular about whipping the eggs vigorously to produce fluffy omelets oozing with molten cheese.

The homemade potato chips were also a performance, and I did eat these. Daddy made crispy potato chips by thinly slicing peeled potatoes. He showed how to place them one-by-one into hot grease to keep them from sticking together and to avoid cooling the grease which produced soggy chips. He got impatient toward the end, placing multiples in the grease, and they tasted delicious, too. In the final step, he salted them generously as they came out of the oil--we didn't worry about sodium in those days. They were delicious because of the ingredients, cooking process, and Daddy being the chef.

A simpler yet delicious breakfast food I associate with Daddy was cinnamon toast. The simple fare needed only white bread, soft margarine to spread on it, cinnamon-sugar mix to sprinkle on it, and a toaster oven for preparing it. Many people had pop-up toasters, but we had the small oven and used it to prepare this modest but yummy treat.

Momma and Daddy used to hug in the kitchen, which made us roll our eyes and groan. The connection between Daddy and Momma strengthened over time. After my brother left for college, I worried "empty nest syndrome" would overcome them but was pleasantly surprised. They spent more time together, traveled, and went on cruises. I treasure the memories of the food and the hugs and appreciate our parents' healthy relationship.

Moping Place

The back steps led from the kitchen through the porch to the backyard. Members of the family and close friends came and went through this entrance as much as through the front. The back steps were a great place to mope when I was unhappy. My dog Prince often joined me there in consolation, especially after Momma chased him away from the clothesline with a broom.

Warm Memories

My favorite place during the winter was in front of the fireplace in the living room. It was the main source of heat in the cold months. There were gas heaters in other rooms, including the bedrooms, but for safety reasons the gas heaters were off during the night, so the bedrooms were often cold. We had blankets, but Daddy added an extra touch to keep us cozy at night. He heated a blanket by holding it open in front of the fireplace and then wrapping one each around me, my brother, and my sister. We scurried to bed wrapped in warmth.

In later times the family got electric blankets on the beds to deal with the cold bedrooms. But somehow the electric blankets, which lay passively on the beds waiting for someone to switch them on, never delivered the same kind of warmth provided by my parent holding the blanket in front of the fireplace and then folding it around me. Years later, after both parents have passed on and as I write and relive these memories, I feel the lasting warmth of the care and love from the fireplace-warmed blanket.

The Beach

Edisto Beach anchors me to South Carolina as my place of origin and home. It occupies a small part of Edisto Island, a barrier sea island off the coast of South Carolina. I spoke my first complete sentence when I first saw the Atlantic Ocean from Edisto Beach: "See there, Daddy, tea." I imagine I was in awe at the large, energetic body of water stretching to the horizon. The ocean, with its wind, waves, and tides, is never standing still.

Our family vacationed at Edisto Beach every summer in July, after the busy farming season ended. A week of pure heaven from a child's point of view, it was the high point of summer and rivaled Christmas as the anticipated event of the year.

Getting There

The drive seemed interminable to my brother, sister, and me. Edisto was an hour from our home outside of Walterboro, a long time in a child's mind especially when gripped by exuberant anticipation. We coped by breaking the trip into mileposts showing progress along the way.

We knew we were getting closer to the coast when we reached the first milestone, Highway 174, a 17-mile stretch of secondary road covered with a Live Oak canopy. This is one of the most scenic routes in South Carolina and features copious amounts of Spanish Moss hanging from the trees. These old trees with crooked trunks and branches, draped in mysterious moss, have weathered many storms. I've often wished I could talk with them about what they have experienced and seen.

The second milestone was reaching the Island. In the early years Edisto Island was connected to the mainland by an electrically powered swing span bridge over the Dawhoo River. This waterway was and still is part of the intracoastal waterways, and sometimes a tall sailboat or large yacht traveled through. This was exciting for the children and frustrating for the adults. Highway traffic came to a stop to allow the bridge to swing open for passage of the waterway vessels. It was quite a sight to see the roadway suspended over and parallel to the waterway to allow ships to move through. We waved enthusiastically to people on any passing vessel.

The McKinley Washington, Jr. Bridge replaced the Dawhoo swing bridge in 1993, providing better traffic flow and access to the Island. The "new" bridge may be less exciting for children than one that opens, but it brings rewards of its own. The graceful mile-long concrete bridge is tall enough that a swing span or drawbridge mechanism is not needed, and it provides a panoramic view of the coastal landscape. You can see the river and creeks winding through marshes for miles.

The coastal wetlands scenery, visible as one crossed onto Edisto Island, puzzled me when I was small. I expected an island to be a small piece of land surrounded by a large body of water, perhaps an ocean, but some of Edisto's enclosing bodies of water were narrow creeks embedded in marshes. This is a characteristic of barrier islands, present on the East and Gulf coasts in the U.S. as well as in other parts of the world. These unique bodies absorb energy from storms, protect coastlines, and create protected marshlands; as a result, they and their shorelines are constantly changing. The salt marshes have a distinctive smell and are teaming with animal and plant life, largely invisible to the casual viewer. This transitional area where rivers meet the sea can range in salinity from near ocean strength to brackish. It is one of the most biologically productive ecosystems on the planet and provides the nursing grounds and habitat for many species of birds and fish.

After arriving on the Island, we had to endure fourteen additional miles before reaching the final milestone. Then, at last, the dense jungle of trees and vegetation on both sides of the road gave way to open saltwater marshes at the same moment the road turned sharply left, suddenly revealing our destination. Known as "the magic curve" to me, my sister, and my brother, this was the final turn into the small town of Edisto Beach. We had arrived!

Being There

Our Edisto family vacations were extravaganzas shared with four families of aunts, uncles, and close friends for a week. Our group rented several nearby houses to accommodate the 21 adults and children, not counting additional visitors who came by for a day of swimming, crabbing, or waterskiing. Some of the rental houses became repeats from year to year. I especially loved the place called "Money Sunk." Like most accommodations on Edisto Beach, it was built on tall stilts as protection from hurricane flooding. We searched for doodlebugs in small cone-shaped pits in the sand under the house.

I never saw a doodlebug and wondered if their existence was a myth perpetuated by adults to get children out of the house. I have since learned they are the larvae of the antlion insect and the sand pits were intended traps for prey such as ants. Perhaps I never saw them because I didn't recite the verse correctly: "Come out doodlebug, your house is on fire…." We spent hours chanting the verse, searching for the elusive bugs and never seemed to tire of it. That is, we looked for them under the house when there was a breeze—without some wind to keep them away, the ever-present mosquitoes "carried us away" on a still summer day at the beach.

Mosquitoes were one of the two unpleasant features of the beach, and there were only two. The other was sandspurs, which were everywhere. It was nearly impossible to walk barefooted, so we wore flip flops all the time. Or we were supposed to. Occasionally one of us tried to sneak across the yard barefooted and, as often as not, got a sandspur deeply embedded in the foot or a toe. Implanted spurs hurt intensely; getting them out was painful, too, and was best done with adult assistance. This surgical task often fell to Daddy who performed admirably under the pressure of operating on a screaming and wriggling child. But mosquitoes and sandspurs were minor annoyances, part of the price for the joy of being at the beach.

I examined patterns of knots in the boarded ceiling of Money Sunk before drifting off to sleep in my daily nap. Counting knots was a good alternative to counting sheep as a sleep aid but this was rarely needed; the beach activities, abundant food, light breezes, and ocean air all contributed to very restful afternoon naps and nighttime sleep. I still remember the sensation in my body at night after daytime swims in the ocean; you felt the waves as though you were standing in waist-high water, even while you were in bed. It was an eerie, yet relaxing, feeling.

Edisto Beach was and still is a family beach with little commercial development. This is another way of saying the main attractions are the Atlantic Ocean, sand, and seashells. In the early days there were plenty of shells, which to me were prizes. I didn't think about the creatures which once occupied them and lost their homes; perhaps they were "trading up." Instead I focused on the details and the beauty: the polish, colors, shapes, and curves. When I was small, I valued only the "perfect" whole shells.

On trips in recent years I've come to appreciate the grace, charm, and mystery of broken shells. Perhaps my own experience of wear due to aging has broadened my understanding of beauty, enabling me to look beyond the outer covering. For many shells, the remarkable hues, contours, and complexity of structure are not visible until the covering is at least partially removed. Or perhaps I became interested in the unknowable life stories of damaged shells. Shells are made of very durable material—what happened to break them? When I go shelling now, I collect broken and partial shells as well as whole shells. I display them in jars, shadow boxes, trays, and frames to honor the unknown histories and natural beauty.

Doing Things

I loved hunting seashells on long beach walks with Aunt Anne, my mother's sister and dutifully learned the names of the shells from her. In retrospect, she did not use the correct names of many shells and made up names to call them. But it didn't matter to me then or now. I think her name, *angel wing,* sounds much more descriptive than the more accurate, *Alternate Tellin.* And a *Knobbed Whelk* will always be a *conch* to me. I was enthralled on these walks. The holy grail of shells was the sand dollar, or *sea biscuit* as we called them. They used to be plentiful—I remember we would often find several in one beach-walking excursion. You can still occasionally find them at Edisto—I now see a whole one once every few years. I still feel as though I have discovered treasure when I find one.

Sometimes I walked on the beach without hunting shells, especially during the teen years and later. I liked to walk from the State Park to Jeremy Inlet separating Edisto and Edingsville Beaches. Edingsville had unusual shells and intricate configurations of changing inlets, and I loved exploring it. The original Edingsville, a once-thriving community, was buried by the 1893 Sea Islands Hurricane; it now lies under the Atlantic and was never rebuilt.

At low tide Jeremy Inlet was shallow and could be crossed it at its narrowest point, but you would be stuck for hours on Edingsville Beach if you tarried while the tide came in. Once I convinced my mother, siblings, and several cousins to cross the Inlet with me at low tide. I kept walking and exploring, delaying the group's return crossing back to Edisto; we had to navigate Jeremy Inlet in chest-high water with strong currents. Momma was not happy. I was often tempted to traverse Edingville to reach the next inlet, Frampton; this required a round-trip jog to beat the tide. I never did this because I feared I couldn't run as fast as needed for as long as needed to make it.

More typically, we enjoyed hanging around the house, playing cards and eating. Everything tasted better at the beach, especially the fresh shrimp. When not eating we spent time at the pavilion with its music, arcade games, pier, and crowds, and in later years we visited the miniature golf course. But the main activity, the reason to go to the beach, was to swim in the ocean.

We looked forward to two swims per day. Most family members had easily sunburned fair skin, so we went on the beach early and late to avoid the harshest sunlight during the middle of the day. It was Daddy's job to monitor all the children and keep us safe when we were in and near the water.

He did this by continuously counting heads. This was no small task, as we were moving targets, walking and running in the shallow water, lounging on inner tubes, splashing in the waves, building castles or digging holes in the sand, and running around on the beach. Daddy was up to it. There was at least one scare, with the count coming one head short. But, fortunately, a cousin had slipped off the beach to return to the house without letting anyone know. Daddy often played the protector role, and he did it very well.

Another wonderful beach activity was waterskiing in Big Bay Creek running off the South Edisto River. Daddy or Uncle Junior usually drove the motorboat, pulling the skiers at the end of ski ropes. Their lighthearted exchanges still ring in my head, "See you later, alligator!" "After 'while, crocodile!" It was a challenge learning to ski, and I remember the thrill when I first got it right: holding onto the ski rope and rising from a crouched position mostly underwater, to the full standing skiing stance, skimming across the surface. It was more like plowing through water, but at the time it felt like flying.

One time when skiing, I looked down and saw a small pod of shiny, dark gray dolphins swimming on both sides of me. It seemed they were deliberately keeping pace with me. My heart beat faster and I had to be sure to keep breathing. I was not afraid for my safety, as their presence felt benevolent, even protective. For those moments I was connected to the dolphins and to the ocean, participating in something much larger than myself. A moment in time, the magic of that memory has stayed with me over the years.

When I visit now, I am amazed we skied in the narrow creek with strong currents and murky water, lined with oyster beds on one side and the marina on the other. But at the time it was great fun and we didn't seem mindful of potential dangers.

I marvel at the amount of hassle and sheer burden of labor these annual beach trips must have been for the adults. We were fortunate as children because everything important was taken care of, mostly below our awareness at the time. From my current adult perspective, I know it was not so simple. In addition to keeping track of about a dozen children, there was planning meals, shopping for food, cooking, or cleaning up from one of the three meals a day; plus, there were the usual tasks of house cleaning, clothes washing, and dealing with the inevitable small emergencies.

We gathered some of our food, as the group went on a crabbing outing during the week. The once-a-year crabbing expedition was supervised by my mother's mother, Grandmother Tulls, who visited us during the week. She was our resident expert on crabbing, having been raised on a neighboring barrier island. We travelled some distance by foot through marshes to get to good crabbing locations at the edges of local saltwater creeks. I remember these expeditions with fondness now, as these were beautiful estuaries teaming with aquatic life and shells. But I imagine at the time we children probably asked repeatedly, "Are we there yet?"

Our version of crabbing had to be one of the lowest tech activities possible. Daddy showed us how to tie the end of a piece of strong cord, maybe 10 feet in length, to a piece of meat; we often used turkey necks. Then, holding on the other end of the cord, we tossed the meat out into the creek. After standing there for a few minutes we slowly pulled in the string. As the meat on the end of the string came into view in the water, we looked for a blue crab, travelling along with the meat and using its claws to pull off and eat bits. When the crab got close enough, a second person with a net scooped up the crab with a deft swoop through the water.

I found another way to catch crabs. With a crab net in hand, I stood barefooted slightly more than ankle deep in the edge of the water and waited. Sooner or later, a crab slowly approached. Before the crab grabbed my foot or toes with a claw, I netted it. I didn't use this technique for long. Maybe an adult stopped me from engaging in this ingenious form of crabbing; or maybe I just came to my senses with a close claw encounter during a brief lapse of attention. Just as well, as I imagine a crab claw pinch is worse than a sandspur for the toes.

Crabbing day ended with a feast featuring Tull's special crab cake delicacy. Before the meal, the adults spent hours picking crab meat from the cooked shells. One of the perks of childhood is being exempt from more tedious and demanding activities such as picking crab meat. But we did partake in eating the delicacy. I almost never order crab cakes in restaurants now. There is simply no way they can compare to those childhood memories.

Growing Up

Edisto feels like home, even though I've visited rather than lived there. Those stays have been regular and throughout my life. In 1975, Colleton County annexed the Town of Edisto Beach, making it part of my home county; this was possible because Edisto Beach and Colleton County are contiguous by water. Edisto Island remained in Charleston County. More importantly, I spent a formative week there every summer during childhood and met my first boyfriend there during my early teens. Like many vacation romances, it was thrilling and short-lived.

My high school and college boyfriends spent time with our family there. The family bought a house in the mid-1970s making frequent visits easier, and around the same time I joined a group of college friends for many enjoyable times on Edisto. I honeymooned there when I married in December 1987; my husband and I visit over the winter holidays to celebrate our anniversary every year.

The things I do at the beach have evolved over the years. As much as I love the ocean, I do not enjoy swimming in it. Even when I was a child and loved to float on an inner tube in the waves, I couldn't wait to get a shower when I got out of the water; saltwater felt sticky and unpleasant on my skin. I haven't gone swimming in the ocean for many years now. I spend hours walking on the beach and collecting shells. I use the shells in crafts and get pleasure sampling the infinite treasures given freely by the sea. It is a reminder that, much like grace, nature's gifts surround us, and we must be open to receive them. I love sitting on the porch listening to the ocean, watching birds, and reading. In retirement years, I've added participating in Edisto Island art retreats. As an artist, I am learning to see one of my favorite places on the planet with fresh eyes.

People tell me they must be on vacation for two weeks before beginning to relax. I feel relaxation flowing through me by the time I reach the island. As in earlier years, wonder flows through me each time I round the magic curve. I sense the island's many habitats, teaming with life. The marshes, ocean air, and perpetually moving ocean permeate my being. Time at Edisto has shaped who I am, and I wouldn't have it any other way. I have joked with friends about going there to reconnect with my primordial origins, but it may not be a joke. It feels as though my strong connection with the ageless ocean originated long before the first time my parents brought me to see it. This is where I feel most alive and linked to all that is.

II

Childhood Imaginings

The world is full of magic things, patiently waiting for our senses to grow sharper.

— W.B. Yeats

The memories and reflections in "Childhood Imaginings" originated in the1950s to early 1960s, the childhood years of my life. I was fascinated by the world and how it worked. For a "Curious Child," everything was interesting including Momma's amazing collection of shoes. The "Childhood Imaginings" story describes my fanciful explanations for things I commonly observed, such as seed pods on vines that just might grow into lizards. Other pieces feature adventures involving people and places that shaped me as a person, as well as the family pet. In the warmer months I enjoyed the bookmobile, vacation Bible school, fishing, family vacations, and in the cooler months I hoped for the rare South Carolina Lowcountry snow and went mistletoe hunting.

My approach to storytelling is inspired by my mother, Ruth J. Saunders, who was a storyteller and writer. Momma wrote humorous stories about family and place during her childhood and her children's early years in her collection, "Low Country Children" (1986). The family still enjoys Momma's never-ending gift. I feel honored to follow in her footsteps and am grateful that she encouraged her curious child.

Curious Child

Children will collect seashells from the beach, and rigorously sort them into types, by color and design. They feel it is important, somewhat, to get it right and, having done so, to keep the result. This kind of personal museum is part of the way we define ourselves, an archive of self, and is not mere covetousness of 'stamp collecting'. Children need to classify things in order to get a grasp upon the world…. This is a means to gain an appreciation of the richness of the environment and our human place within it.

— *Life. An Unauthorized Biography*,
Richard Fortey

I arrived in this world at 4:20 am on January 6, 1952, the first of three baby-boom generation children born to my parents. I cried nearly every night for the first two years of my life, except when a hurricane blew the roof off the kitchen. Perhaps I needed background noise to help me sleep. The family physician prescribed Paregoric to ease my discomfort, but it had the opposite effect, making me more agitated. Prior to my birth, Momma, by her own confession, was expecting me to behave like a doll baby. I must have been a rude awakening.

There are pictures of me peeking out from behind Momma's skirt as a toddler--sensitive, imaginative, and tuned into my inner world, I was happiest playing alone or with one or two other close persons. Due to my reticence, it was difficult for me to read out loud when I started school, and I stumbled in front of my peers, though my comprehension was good. Children at this age are not known for their empathy, and many classmates as well as teachers labeled my difficulty reading in public as "slowness." Even with good grades, I felt slow well into high school.

Surrounded by nature, I lived in world rich with ideas and imagination--a place where my curious and inventive mind would thrive. My sister and I, just two years apart in age, spent hours playing pretend games when we were little. One game, called *Parade,* involved four roles, Princess and Parade, as well as a Good Guy and Bad Guy. I played Princess and Good Guy, and my sister was Parade and Bad Guy. In a typical scenario Good Guy rescues Princess, which required a great deal of creativity since I was rescuing myself. We included our brother, four years younger than my sister, when he became old enough. My sister and I had tea parties and dressed him up as a girl, a pretend game he loved. He also liked playing the part of a puppy. I feared we had warped him at a tender age, but we prepared him well for a future life with his wife and three daughters.

I was well understood by my second-grade teacher, Mrs. Peach Foster, though I didn't realize it at the time. When it came time for the annual class-room play in which all children were plants in a garden, she assigned me the part of "Petunia in the Onion Patch," because I often seemed serious and sad. At the time I felt embarrassed to be different. Now I appreciate how she saw me as a flower, and I am thankful for her efforts to support me. In later grades, I refused to take speaking parts in school plays due to my timidity. My mother accepted my hesitancy as one of my curious features.

By grade 2, I preferred reading nonfiction, especially science books. From these I learned observation was a scientist's main tool. I was good at this and decided to be a scientist. I didn't need to wait until adulthood to take up my chosen profession—I had already started. I became fascinated with atoms and atomic particles and learned all I could about protons, neutrons, and electrons. An observer captivated by things too small to be seen, I saw them clearly in my mind's eye.

I now know my childhood understanding of the building blocks of matter was simplified. An entire field is devoted to the study of particle physics, and sci-entists have identified an array of subatomic particles—quarks, leptons, gluons, photons, and bosons of different sorts. I am not able to wrap my brain around this complexity but still try to understand the strange microworld underlying what we call reality.

My inward tendency was counterbalanced by curiosity, which compelled me to explore the world around me. I investigated objects like insects, leaves, seeds, shells and especially rocks, which I collected, organized, and labeled. I pictured myself as a scientific explorer and entered my best collection in an elementary school science fair. The specimens were magnificent, at least to my eyes, and I could not believe I didn't win a prize for my discoveries. Admittedly, my collecting expeditions were not adventurous—my rocks were conveniently located in the ballast that supported the railroad tracks running through the field by the house. Still, I worked hard to select the best examples among the piles of crushed rock.

My collections, along with the names of the rocks, have long been lost. Perhaps they were returned to the track with assistance from my mother. I probably found granite, trap rock, quartzite, dolomite, and limestone, because they are commonly available in southeastern quarries. Many of the rocks contained small plant and animal fossils, imprints of life from the distant past. In retrospect, maybe the fossils would have been a better science fair project.

My parents purchased small rock collections for me when we visited the mountains. These professional displays of exotic rocks were never as satisfying as my personal assemblages because the joy was in finding, organizing, and labeling the rocks myself. With the help of books, I peered into the geologic past to see the earth in a new light and traveled through time to visit earlier forms of life with the fossils. Collecting rocks was a solid beginning to my journey as a scientist.

Gradually, a fascination with biology replaced my geologic passions. I captured bugs, worms and lizards, showed them to my mother, and then released them with her encouragement. Once I excitedly showed her a new and intriguing worm—Momma immediately identified it as a small rattlesnake and quickly got it away from me. I spent hours studying tadpoles, minnows and water bugs in the canal by the field. Bumblebees, moths, and butterflies visiting flowers in the yard were subjected to my scientific examination. The first sighting of a Luna moth, perched on the pumphouse, remains clearly in my mind. The clothespins on the backyard clothesline were perfect perches for sunning dragonflies, known as "mosquito-hawks" to us. With their multi-part, translucent wings, they seemed to be marvels of design as well as works of art.

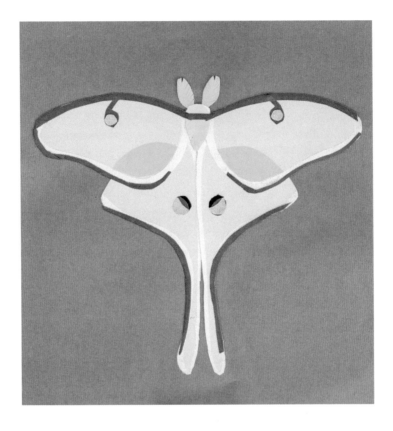

In the sixth grade, I earned enough points in a school-sponsored magazine sale to get a microscope, which opened a miniature realm of existence. A drop of "clear" water contained amoebae, paramecia, and some unidentifiable creatures. This was another example of there being more to the world than met the eye. I wondered if these creatures could sense my presence and if I seemed like a giant to them. My new collection consisted of slides—thin slices of life on glass, preserved and cataloged. But I couldn't stay in an indoor "laboratory" for too long—there was too much to see outdoors. My interest in biology shifted to observing animals, especially the domesticated critters on our farm.

Chicken behavior was baffling to me—some of them were mean and picked on a few unfortunate hens. I felt sorry for weaklings but didn't understand why they didn't stand up for themselves. Much later I learned about social hierarchies in flocks of domesticated fowl, also known as the "pecking order." These social structures maintain order within a flock and determine access to food. I wanted them to treat each other as friends, but these early lessons helped me understand that nature follows its own rules. It was also good training for understanding organizational hierarchies in the work world later in life.

I tried to teach chickens to walk up an incline from the ground to the coop. This enterprise was an unequivocal failure. Even if the board were baited with chicken feed, they simply jumped to the ground. With the hubris of a young scientist, I concluded hens were not smart and switched my training efforts to a more intelligent animal, the cat. This was not a wise choice. The feline trials had the same result as those with domesticated fowl. My conclusion was that cats *didn't want* to walk the plank.

The most puzzling animals of all were people. With most creatures, scientists must learn from observation, but with human beings it is possible to ask questions. My first questionnaire to collect data had one question and was taped to the refrigerator, my mother being the single intended participant. The question was: "To Momma: Do you love me? ____ Yes ____ No. From: Ruthie." Many years would pass before I would learn to avoid emotionally laden questions and to provide more than two answer choices. But never mind that, because I got the response I desired: Momma checked "yes." A future survey researcher was in the making. In my academic life years later, I collected data using questionnaires and taught courses on constructing them. I did not always get the expected response from survey participants in the later years.

By middle school, I looked forward to the new school year and what I would learn. In late summer I reviewed textbooks from the previous year to prepare. My mother found this curious but had become accustomed to my unique approach. In high school, I preferred doing homework to cruising around town, which was the favored social activity among my peers. My peers and siblings became adept at the social skill of recognizing individuals traveling in cars, but not me. To this day I identify automobiles by color and size and know whose car it is from the license plate number. Over the years I have inadvertently slighted acquaintances for failing to recognize them on the road.

Daddy joked that I was going to be a nuclear physicist. He didn't mean it literally; this was his way of acknowledging my scientific leanings. By the time I graduated from high school in spring 1970, I had explored physical, geologic, life, and behavioral sciences through play, reading, and schoolwork. New opportunities lay ahead in college at Clemson University. I initially selected an English major with a Psychology minor. Then, lacking only a course in English history for my major, I flipped the major to Psychology and minor to English. I loved literature and writing but my curiosity drew me toward studying behavior and experimental psychology.

In college I looked like a hippie with long straight hair, bell bottom jeans and home-made tie-dyed t-shirts but was as straight as they came. My sister, who entered Clemson two years later, and I speculated we were the only college students of the era who never tried drugs. Many students took speed to cram for exams all night, but my approach was more natural, relying upon innate anxiety about getting high marks to keep me awake to study. I attended class, studied hard, and earned good grades, with only one "C" my entire four years, ironically in "Creative Writing."

A professor who was successful in research and publishing early in his career hired me to work part-time on his grant. He was an animal behaviorist in the Zoology Department studying bird migration. My job was to manage his large and growing collection of article reprints before the days of electronic files, as well as to assist with office tasks and conferences sponsored by his grant on bird and jet airplane collisions. I learned a lot on the job and admired the professor who was competent, ethical, hard-working, and fair. He liked students, had a great sense of humor, was a bit irreverent in a good way, and was my model for how to be a professor in later years. His class in animal behavior was one of the most influential courses I took as an undergraduate.

The course included an enlightening lab. Working in teams, we performed and wrote up a series of experiments. One of these remain clearly in my memory. We were given two vials, one with male and one with female fruit flies. The procedure was simple: place the open ends of the vials together and wait for flies to mingle and do what comes naturally. It wasn't long before the action started. We timed how long each pair copulated. It was a long lab session because some of them were at it for upwards of 30 minutes.

At some point the fruit fly porn got old. My interest shifted from watching fruit flies to watching my peers watch fruit flies. It was amusing to see young adults clustered, heads together observing intently as tiny insects had sex, but it was hilarious to witness the cheers and shouts of celebration for fly sexual achievement. I wondered how much vicarious pleasure my classmates were experiencing. Perhaps we were spending too much time in the lab.

People convinced me over the years I would have to grow up one day, which meant setting the curious child aside. Graduation from Clemson in 1974 seemed the expected time to "put away childish things," get serious, and start a career. I was uncertain about the direction, but my college grades were good, so I went to graduate school as the first step. From that false start, involving serious study of reptile behavior, I learned that uncertainty about what you want to be when you grow up is a poor reason for starting a PhD program. It took a few years, several jobs that didn't "fit," three graduate programs, and two graduate degrees before I made the biggest discovery of my life: I didn't have to grow up or abandon the curious child to earn a living!

There is a setting that nurtures the curious child, a place that employs many people like me: academia. My career home was in academic public health. In this setting I was paid to be curious, explore ideas, teach, and write about what I had learned. Momma was proud of the published papers in the same way she appreciated my rock collections or shells I found on the beach. My teaching and research in public health may as well have been nuclear physics as far as Daddy was concerned, and he was happy for me. It may seem my profession changed more than once but it was a seamless progression for a curious child who wanted to observe and understand the world and behavior of creatures in it.

The answers I have found have just served to raise a whole new set of questions. In some ways I am as confused as ever, but I believe I am confused on a much higher level and about more important things.

—*Author Unknown*

Childhood Imaginings

Purple hysteria breaks out in early spring in South Carolina, forming cascades of sweetly scented lavender flowers in the shape of grape clusters. You see it in yards and wooded roadsides, in urban and rural areas. Most people call this flowering vine "wisteria." It is an early and exuberant flower that erupts rather than blooms, casting its potent fragrance all over its surroundings. Or maybe I am the hysterical one, elated because I know warmer weather is on the way.

I've enjoyed purple hysteria every spring since childhood. It didn't grow in our yard, but it did grow around trees in the yard of my childhood best friend where I spent much time. I was intrigued by the spiraling flower petals and sturdy vines.

I have since learned purple hysteria is not a single species of plant. Two Asian species of wisteria, Chinese and Japanese, are common in the Eastern U.S., along with the native Atlantic type. They are similar but the Asian species are invasive. I felt the vines were everywhere, taking over the landscape, and perhaps they were.

Purple hysteria delivers a surprise a few months later. In the summer it produces lizard-shaped pods that hang down from the vine. As a child I imagined these pods metamorphized into lizards by developing heads, legs, and tails. They escaped from the vine when ready and scurried away as free lizards. I didn't expect to witness this and not just because it happened only at night. I knew this was my active imagination; the inspiration came from watching tadpoles grow into would-be toads. I never witnessed tadpoles making the transition from water to become land-based amphibians either, although

it is easier to explain animal-to-animal metamorphosis than plant-to-animal transformation.

Wisteria are in the bean family of plants, also known as legumes. The pods are the plant's fruit and contain seeds. One puzzle about the lizard pods from childhood was solved by learning about the different species. The pods on some vines were fuzzy, velvety to the touch but on other vines they were smooth. As a child I pretended the distinctive pods produced different kinds of lizards even though I'd never seen a hairy lizard. The velvety pods were Asian, and the smooth ones were Atlantic.

There was another summertime transformation I imagined in my youth. While the lizard pods were clinging to their vines our family went to Edisto Beach for a week. Summer thunderstorms were common and stunning to

watch if they happened over the ocean. Once, lightning struck the ocean, and I witnessed the instantaneous transformation of the water by 300 million volts of electricity spreading horizontally over the sea's surface. The vast amount of heat and light changed the water into a multicolored polished substance for an instant before it reverted to sea. I wondered how something so powerful could just disappear.

The next day I went for a walk on the beach. The lightning-struck ocean image was on my mind when I spotted many purple-brown stiff pen shells strewn over the sand. Their iridescent metallic inner shell linings glimmered in the sunlight. Stiff pen shells are wedge-shaped filter-feeding mollusks. They attach to rocks or shells in shallow and sandy ocean bottoms and may wash ashore in storms. But never mind that—I understood the lightning strike had created a thin, iridescent sheet of electricity which solidified on the cooler ocean surface and shattered into thousands of shards before washing ashore, and in my hands, I held frozen lightning.

Summer Pastimes

Summers during childhood meant bookmobile visits and Vacation Bible School, both eagerly anticipated. Vacation Bible School (VBS) took place shortly after school ended and was held during the day rather than in the evening as many VBSs do today. I looked forward to the predictable routines, such as lining up to march into the church sanctuary each day and the piano musical cues for the group to sit down and stand up. For refreshments we had Kool Aid and store-bought cookies; these were ordinary fare, but we enjoyed them outside under the picnic shed, which made it special.

I wish I could say Bible study was the highlight of VBS for me, but I was there for the arts and crafts. One craft project used old coffee cans to create decorative containers. We glued three clothespins to the bottom for legs and pasta onto the sides to create "artistic" designs. It came together when sprayed with metallic gold paint. I see something tacky when I review the final product in my adult mind's eye, but to the child's eye it was an elegant work of art. It was the beginning of my lifelong love and practice of creating handicrafts.

The bookmobile came every two weeks during the summer; I returned books I'd read and picked up a new pile. I don't remember specific titles, but I do recall looking down the rural highway for the arrival of my version of the "magic school bus" and the excitement of walking up the short stairs into the large van lined with shelves of books and picking out reading adventures. The selections were limited by most standards, but my love of books and libraries began with the bookmobile.

Aquatic Adventure

It doesn't take much imagination to know the outcome of my first and only fly-fishing lesson in a boat: I hooked Daddy in the back. In the long view, no harm was done, and it is amusing now. But it was not funny on that hot summer afternoon when Daddy's bellows of pain echoed across the pond.

Daddy loved to fish and was quite an expert at fly fishing in the plentiful Lowcountry freshwater ponds. In my preteen years I rowed the boat so he could fish. He had specialized equipment including flyrod and reel, and a variety of lures, but that was just the beginning. The key to *successful* fly fishing is the art of casting the line in graceful arcs through the air and landing the lure precisely at a selected spot on the pond surface. If done properly, the line whispers through the air and gently places the lure in the water, much as an aquatic insect would land.

I remember how Daddy used to whip the line through the air and place the lure on the pond surface with extraordinary grace. He then pulled the line in short, rapid jerks moving the lure over the water's surface, simulating a live insect moving over the water. This, of course, was designed to convince a fish to consume what appeared to be an ordinary meal.

After the fish fell for the bait, Daddy set the hook, reeled the fish in, and netted it into the boat. Catching fish by fly fishing can go wrong in so many ways: incorrect bait, poor technique with casting or retrieving the fish, and equipment failure such as the line breaking, to name a few. And some days they just aren't biting. These accumulated challenges are, in part, what creates the reward and excitement when the prize fish is caught. Daddy was rewarded frequently.

If having a great model were all it took, I would be an expert at fly fishing. And I did well enough when I practiced in the yard. It's one thing to cast a long line ending in a sharp hook on dry land. It's quite another to do it while two people are sitting in close quarters in a small rowboat. It didn't take me long; I cast the line forward, flicked it behind me, and coming forward again the line dipped too low, hooking Daddy in the middle of his back.

This event was so stressful that I don't remember how I removed the hook. Daddy probably stopped hollering long enough to talk me through cutting off the head of the hook to remove it with minimal damage to his back. He didn't invite me to sling dangerous hooks through the air after the hook-in-back incident, but I continued to paddle the boat for him.

Earlier days of pole fishing with Daddy didn't bode well for my future fishing, either. The equipment was very basic: a line tied to a pole with a fishhook on the free end. We used live earthworms or crickets to bait the hooks. I did not like impaling the live creatures on the hook and got Daddy to do it for me. How ironic.

A floating cork was attached to the line above the fishhook, and the baited hook was lowered into the water. When a fish nibbled at the bait, the cork bobbed in the water's surface. If the fish took the bait, it usually got hooked and the cork disappeared underwater. I liked seeing the cork bob and could wait patiently for hours to catch a glimpse. I got very excited when the cork disappeared. Apparently, I lost my deep sense of empathy for the bait creature as soon as it was out of sight underwater. It was replaced by empathy for the fish once it had been hooked. I did not like removing the hook from the fish and got Daddy to do that, too.

Except for the time I caught Daddy, I enjoyed the time I spent fishing with him. I believe he did, too. But it was not my destiny to follow in my father's fishing footsteps. These father-daughter outings stopped in my teens when I began bringing a radio into the boat so I could listen to my favorite artists: Jimmy Ruffin, the Box Tops, and the Four Tops. I don't think Daddy minded it so much, but the music disturbed the fish. And, as anyone who fishes knows, that just won't do.

Momma's Shoes

My mother always had a closet full of shoes, a source of fascination to me from early childhood. There was every kind of shoe one can imagine: athletic shoes including walking shoes, running shoes, tennis shoes; sandals of all shapes and descriptions including multiple pairs of flip-flops; casual shoes to wear around the house; dress shoes with low heels and high heels; and various pairs of bedroom shoes in a variety of conditions from well-worn, in fact barely recognizable as shoes, to pristine princess slippers. The variety in colors was amazing, but I will say Momma kept the styles very basic. No elaborate sequins, buckles, or glitter. She was a no-frills woman, and I'm proud to say that I have taken after her in that respect.

Some of these shoes fit the many roles she played. She worked while raising children and was a professional legal secretary before helping Daddy run his business. She was also an elected school board official and served as chair of the board for many years; acted as surrogate mother to my friends; engaged actively in community life; and was a writer in her spare time—she wrote local histories and self-published a book of family stories. If something needed to be done, Momma did it. That included everything from cooking, changing diapers, sewing clothes, and serving as a Cub Scout Den Mother to refinishing wood floors and laying brick around the base of the house. My mother was an incredible role model, far ahead of her time.

Momma was also a generous woman and frequently gave shoes away. She maintained her large shoe inventory by constantly buying new shoes. In fact, every time she went shopping for anything, she checked out the shoe sales. And as often as not, she came home with another pair of shoes. As I grew older, I assumed that my mother had a "thing" for shoes. Maybe something like a shoe obsession, but not one serious enough to require some type of diagnosis. Plus, she kept them in the closet rather than scattered about the house, which could've been a hazard. And because she was a bargain hunter and didn't spend excessive amounts of money, it seemed harmless enough and occasionally amusing.

With this voluminous number of shoes, it is no surprise that my mother rarely went barefooted. She had some type of shoe for every occasion including some occasions that had not arisen yet. Of course, it's best to be prepared and, when it came to shoes, she was. Even though they were typically covered, I admired my mother's feet from early childhood. I thought they were beautiful. They were both rounded and angular in odd ways that make her feet quite unique. I believed that this was something to be proud of and was surprised that she constantly had her feet covered with a pair of shoes. I was always happy to get a peek at her feet.

As I became older, I discovered that I had inherited my mother's feet. I also found out that feet are not particularly intended to be uniquely rounded and angular in odd ways. It turns out the cause of this external beauty, as I saw it in early childhood, is severe bunions and osteoarthritis. In other words, my mother's feet hurt. They hurt all the time. In middle age as I pondered my foot fate with inheriting my mother's uniquely and oddly rounded and angular feet, I also began sharing some of her pain. But that's okay, I feel like I am following in amazing footsteps. It's a small price to pay.

It wasn't too long ago that I had another realization about my mother's feet and her shoes. She didn't have a "thing" for shoes at all. She was simply searching for a comfortable pair of shoes that didn't hurt her feet. Apparently, judging from the collection in her shoe closet, she never found them. In recent years, I've taken up my mother's quest for finding a comfortable pair of shoes. I am amassing a nice collection as I continue this ongoing search and carry forward my mother's foot legacy. I know, though, that I will never be able to "fill her shoes." There were simply too many of them.

Hills and Mountains

My first sight of a mountain in North Carolina around age 11 was a wondrous experience. I couldn't believe how the land rose up and was framed by the sky. Our family made many trips to the Blue Ridge Mountains of South Carolina, Georgia, and North Carolina during the years my sister, brother, and I were growing up. We visited the Great Smoky Mountain National Park; National Forests including Pisgah, Nantahala, and Chattahoochee-Oconee; and numerous State Parks in all three states. We enjoyed the natural sights of trees and mountains as well as the tourist attractions or, as my father called them, the tourist "traps." These trips have merged in my mind as one, large, happy memory, much as individual mountains in a large, interconnected chain become one.

The Blue Ridge Mountains are part of the larger Appalachian Mountain Range; they extend 550 miles from southern Pennsylvania through Maryland, West Virginia, Virginia, North Carolina, South Carolina, Tennessee, and Georgia. These ancient mountains have been worn down by the elements for hundreds of millions of years, so they lack the tall peaks prominent in the Rocky Mountains of the Western United States. Mount Elbert in Colorado is the tallest peak in the Rockies at 14,440 feet. In contrast, Mount Mitchell in North Carolina boasts the highest summit in the Blue Ridge range at 6,684 feet. The Smokies may have been eroded by weather over time, but for youngsters who had experienced only the Lowcountry of South Carolina they were *serious* mountains. We were raised in Colleton County, which is a large swamp with flat agricultural fields and pine forests interspersed throughout.

To put our awe at first seeing the Smokies in perspective, consider Daddy's field known as "The Big Hill." The name suggests elevated terrain with a visible rise. But visitors to the area were bewildered by what they saw: a flat 40-acre field. Its name reflected a notable Lowcountry fact: it was *several inches above* the surrounding swamps. Yes, the Smokies were big!

In the summer we would seek out waterfalls and places to hike. We walked on paths to reach high overlooks with expansive views and to get to rivers at lower elevations. Momma was nervous about the overlooks and did not want us to get close to the edge. My attitude was more nonchalant, and I pushed as close to the precipice as possible. This predictably resulted in an apprehensive mother. I could not understand why she made a big deal out of it. When I visited years later, my nonchalant attitude about the steep drop-offs was replaced by sheer terror and approaching the edge was unthinkable. I now have retroactive empathy for my mother and a better appreciation of her concerns.

The mountains were adorned in textures of many greens in the summer, and in the fall, hardwood leaves transformed themselves into bright oranges, reds, yellows, golds, and purples. You could see miles into the distance on a clear day—it was more three-dimensional than the restricted visibility afforded by flat land. I took many pictures of mountain landscapes—and few pictures of the people who enjoyed them.

One of our favorite destinations was Sliding Rock, a natural waterfall enjoyed as a giant sliding board in the Pisgah National Forest. It was exciting being propelled by the shallow water rushing down the smooth, sloping rock into a calm pool. In my mind, I can feel myself moving through the cool stream and warm air, hear the rushing water, and smell the uplands vegetation. Repeating the slide more than a couple of times required reinforced-bottom bathing suit bottoms or multiple layers of shorts, because the rock-slide generated eroding friction on the fabric.

Another repeat destination was Looking Glass Falls, also in the Pisgah National Forest. We hiked a short trail to its base to view the single 60-foot drop from below. I loved the water spray and deep moisture. Magnificent moss and deep green plants of many varieties grew on the surrounding rock outcroppings.

I was fascinated by the rivers, with clear water running over smooth rocks. I loved to wade, though you had to be careful not to slip. I marveled at the fish you could see swimming in them. This was quite a contrast to the tannic, slow-moving Lowcountry creeks and rivers. Many of the mountain streams looked creek-sized to me, but they became larger as they gathered water through miles of decreasing elevations on their timeless journey toward the sea.

Over the years, we stayed in motels, a friend's cabin, and the family camper. We youngsters liked the motels and the cabin but had mixed feelings about the camper. It had a chemical smell, likely due to its self-contained nature including a restroom. We complained a lot, but the family had invested in it, so we used it. In retrospect, it was an adventure to stay in the camper, and I wish I could retract some of those earlier complaints.

Lodging served as a base for outings and was not the main destination. But one of my favorite memories was from the first motel on the first trip. I was impressed by the variety of individually packaged jellies and jams served at breakfast, especially flavors beyond grape and apple. To this day, I delight in individually packaged marmalade, apple butter and blackberry jam on toast or English muffins. Small things can create a lifetime of pleasures.

My recent mountain trips have been to the Pisgah National Forest on the Blue Ridge Parkway. I remain in awe of the overwhelming dimensionality when I see the rows of rounded peaks; size and color recede into the distance. I find the wildflowers, plants, tress, and streams as intriguing as the first time I saw them. But the sense of adventure and excitement remain with the memories of childhood. Being in the presence of nature now brings peace and the knowledge that I can return to the vacations of childhood at the mountains or beach at any time through reminisces.

Sandy McDonald Saunders

Sandy McDonald Saunders, a blonde shepherd mix, became a member of our family in the mid-1960s after being exiled from his first community. He began pethood with the McDonald family in the town of Walterboro. My brother, sister, and I knew Sandy as his first home was situated behind our grandmother Tulls' place. He was renowned in her neighborhood, and not in a good way—Tulls often complained about "that nuisance of a dog." At the time I thought he was just full of life.

Sandy expressed his *joie de vivre* by digging in gardens, a serious offense from my plant-loving grandmother's point-of-view, and by moving loose objects around the neighborhood. He routinely collected the newspapers delivered to yards and porches. Without their daily and weekly papers, residents missed out on small town news and gossip from community and church columns; after all, keeping up with reunions and revivals was one of the rewards of small-town living.

Once, I witnessed Sandy's prowess in action. One of Tulls' neighbors worked under his car parked on the street. He periodically slid out from under the car on a creeper, took a few sips of Coke from a bottle which he had set by the car, and then slid back under the car. Sandy observed for a time. Then, with calculated precision, he padded up to the car while the man was under it, gently grasped the Coke bottle by the neck, and carried it off. I was so amused by this I didn't report it because I did not want to get Sandy in trouble yet another time. I don't know what the dog did with it, but I don't believe he drank the soda. He was not after the soft drink; he just liked to pick things up and take them away, perhaps a form of canine kleptomania or a "retrieve gene" gone awry. As far as I know, no one ever found his cache of collected treasures.

I cannot remember the final transgression that got Sandy expelled from town, but my sister, brother, and I were delighted because he came to live with us in the country. He instantly became a sixth member of the family. Out of respect for his first family we dubbed him "Sandy McDonald Saunders," the only family pet honored with a first, middle, and last name. He had always been a country dog at heart; his playful nature was not a problem in our spacious rural community which had places, children, and other critters to check out and play with. He rode in the car with us and was the first family pet allowed to stay indoors. Momma had a dog from before she married, a black Cocker Spaniel named "Sugar," also granted house privileges. But Sugar was a grumpy old dog, not child-friendly, and was *Momma's* pet.

There were certain people Sandy picked on. One of them was the lady that came to the house to help my mother with cleaning and ironing. He would bark ferociously while running toward her, and as he reached her he jumped, snapping his jaws in the air as he sailed by, nearly shoulder high. This display did not phase her in the least; she simply said "Sandy, you make me so sick." He didn't like her, but I don't believe he meant her any harm; it was all a game to him.

Sandy was the life of the party at family celebrations, birthdays, holidays, and gatherings; everybody looked forward to seeing him. For Halloween parties we dressed him in a costume. It didn't matter which person was the guest of honor—Sandy was always the center of attention.

Sandy enjoyed people food in addition to the routine fare dog food, and we're not talking about table scraps. He had exacting tastes; he savored a home-made waffle, but only if it was covered with both syrup and sour cream. I don't remember the exact ingredients to his preferred made-to-order omelet. Yes, this dog was spoiled. Every member of the family loved him, and he loved us.

One Christmas morning my brother, sister, Sandy and I exuberantly piled into a bed intended for one. The spirited throng of three-children-with-dog-in-small-bed was our way of coping Tulls' watchful eye on Christmas mornings. She spent Christmas Eve with us when we were young and kept a vigil from her bed to prevent us from sneaking into the living room early to see what Santa had delivered. We couldn't tell if she didn't sleep or if superb hearing awoke her when any one of us set a foot on the floor. Tulls served as an after-the-fact Santa's helper, keeping us at bay until our parents roused and witnessed the joyful chaos of Christmas mornings around the Saunders' family Christmas tree. I still feel the closeness and hear the laughter from that morning.

If he got sick or injured, Sandy got priority care as a family member. One day I had a sore throat but not a bad one; the family discussed whether I should visit a doctor. This discussion was cut short by Sandy's snakebite crisis. In one of his outdoor adventures, a rattlesnake bit him on the leg which immediately quadrupled in size. My health issues faded into the background as we rallied to deal with the canine family member emergency. Fortunately, Momma got him to the vet immediately and he recovered.

Life in the country provided autonomy for free-spirited canines who were poor fits for an urban setting. But the snakebite was a reminder of the cost of freedom. One ever-present danger was greater than snakes: traffic moving 55 mph or faster on the farm-to-market road in front of our house. This hazard was amplified if the animal liked chasing vehicles. Sandy didn't chase cars, but he had a fondness for pursuing trucks and nipping at the tires, especially if they slowed down and sped up. We received milk deliveries at home, so milk trucks regularly stopped by the house and, being a farm, many trucks came and went. We did everything we could to break Sandy of his truck-chasing habit, but it made no difference. His urge to chase, like his urge to collect objects, was part of his irrepressible nature.

The milk truck was Sandy's ultimate undoing. No one in the family witnessed the event, but while in pursuit, he bit a moving tire which broke his neck. He did not suffer and, as far as we know, death was instantaneous. Sandy McDonald Saunders was buried in the family pet cemetery behind the barn. We had lost a family member, playmate, friend, and force of nature, opening a void in our lives that could not be filled. The raw pain ran deep but the five members of our family never grieved together in public. Instead, each of us went alone to the gravesite behind the barn and cried in private. Each of us believed he or she was the only person struggling. It was some time before we talked about it and discovered that each of us had dealt with our grief in separate but similar ways.

Fifty years later, I feel Sandy's absence, though the passage of time has diminished the pain. In its place are sweet remnants of his infectious joy for living. We became better people for having known Sandy McDonald Saunders and our world became a better place for his having been part of it.

South Carolina Snow

Snow is rare in Colleton County and when it does snow, it is a big deal. Daddy once woke me, my sister and brother up in the early hours of the morning when it was dark and snowing. Snow wouldn't fall or remain on the ground for long and he wanted us to see it. It was exhilarating going from slumber to stumbling sleepiness to white magic.

In the early years it was safe to eat the snow. Momma or Daddy collected clean snow and sweetened and flavored it with vanilla; I can't remember the recipe. But I do remember that it was delicious: the original snow cone. A typical South Carolina snowfall accumulated less than one inch and would be gone by midday. Somehow, we still made snowmen, threw snowballs, and collected and ate snow, which no doubt contributed to its rapid disappearance.

On one of the heavier snows, probably three inches, my best friend and I decided to make a large snowman in her yard. The plan was to make it in three stacked sections, with the base the largest and the head the smallest. Our ambitions were greater than our abilities. We worked together and rolled a ball of snow for the base—until it was so large and heavy that the two of us could not move it to the chosen spot. We then realized that the two of us could not roll and lift the remaining sections to build the snowman, so we abandoned the project. The reminder of our failed project persisted for the weeks it took the large and tightly packed ball of snow to melt.

When the weather forecast mentions the "S" word in South Carolina, bread and milk vanish from the shelves of the grocery store. Snow shuts people into their homes mainly because the roads are unsafe to travel. There are no snowplows and South Carolinians have little experience driving in winter weather conditions. Ice storms are worse because in addition to hazardous highway conditions, ice accumulates on wires and trees that fall on wires, shutting power down. This makes preserving the refrigerator full of milk challenging, but there is plenty of bread to eat.

The rare and scant Stokes snowfalls didn't stop Daddy from telling stories about his childhood hardship of walking miles to school through heavy accumulations of snow. It was true that he walked to school, as he attended the Stokes community school prior to going to Walterboro High School, but it was less than a mile walk. I hope I didn't fall for the part about the heavy snowfall, though I probably felt a little sorry for him even if I didn't buy the snow story. I'm certain that he sometimes had to walk to school with heavy frost on the ground.

Mistletoe Hunting

Ido not like firearms. I fired one once when I was growing up, and only then because an adult "helped" me through the process. That was the last time. But desperate times require drastic measures, and surely the search for "perfect" Christmas decorations qualifies as a time of grave need. Plus, shooting mistletoe out of trees for Christmas is a time-honored and customary Southern USA tradition. And daddy had both the gun and the boat for the job.

During my pre-teen to teen years I was obsessed with decorating the house for Christmas. The decorations were ordinary arrangements of greens with red berries, pinecones, figurines, candles on the fireplace mantle, and any open surfaces I could find in the house. I hung bobbles and sparkling strands from doorframes and from nails tacked into convenient places from earlier decorating efforts. And, of course, it would not have been complete without the addition of something special: mistletoe. I hung bunches of it at strategic locations over doorways throughout the house. I was not content with artificial greenery. No, it *had* to be authentic.

Enter Daddy. I always enlisted him to help me get the magic greenery, typically growing very high in trees near our rural home. Plus, the healthiest bunches were in trees surrounded by water in a Lowcountry swamp. Retrieving it was not for the faint-of-heart. Daddy undertook this task due to a combination of fatherly love for his daughter and my remarkable insistence on getting it done; he did not care about Christmas decorations.

Getting the mistletoe down involved having the right equipment and several challenging maneuvers. A boat was needed to deal with the swamp; getting a boat into the swamp and then yourself into the boat while holding a firearm was no simple task. But that alone doesn't get you much closer to the prize; to bridge the vertical distance gap, a shotgun and ammunition were needed to shoot it down. The fallen treasure must be retrieved from wherever it fell into the swamp. Then you had to reverse the process to get it safely out.

So, the mistletoe-gathering ritual went something like this: Daddy and I vigorously negotiated how to get the boat into the swamp and to get Daddy safely in the boat without getting wet, while he held a shotgun. We disagreed on nearly every point from where the boat should go in to how best to hold the shotgun. Next, Daddy navigated the boat around stumps and fallen debris in the swamp for the best angle to shoot the green gem down while I coached from the sidelines. After carefully aiming, Daddy fired the shotgun toward the green target as I looked the other way with my hands over my ears. Daddy would then navigate the boat to retrieve the greenery while I called out helpful hints from the edge of the water, which he did not seem to interpret as "helpful" in the least. Daddy successfully got himself and the gun out of the boat onto dry land and pulled the boat out of the swamp, while I continued to provide supportive suggestions. Finally, he handed me the hard-won prize. The Christmas miracle was that we remained on speaking terms.

My insistence on strategically hanging sprigs of fresh mistletoe around the house at Christmastime never resulted in a kiss from any person, special or otherwise, and the family dog doesn't count. But that was not the real intent. At the time I believed that the Yuletide green contributed to the "perfect Christmas," an elusive and idealized image of what Christmases should be. I believed concrete symbols, such as fresh greenery hanging in all doorways in the house, gave presence to the promise of Christmas: hope, love, and peace.

In later years, perhaps with more perspective, I understood elaborate hunting rituals and perfect decorations were not required; the hope of Christmas lives within one and is best expressed through actions toward other people throughout the year. Like getting in a boat in a swamp in the winter and shooting mistletoe out of a tree for one's daughter.

To this day, decades after the years of hanging mistletoe have passed, I still scan the landscape for trees with the familiar green clusters as the holidays approach. And I think of Daddy and how he helped build the foundations for my sustained sense of hope for humankind.

III

Driven to Distraction

Men do not quit playing because they grow old; they grow old because they quit playing.

— Oliver Wendell Holmes Sr.

The reminisces in "Driven to Distraction" originated after childhood, during the late 1960s and beyond. Family and friends commented on my serious nature when I was small. What they didn't realize was that I had peaked and plateaued on staidness by age 10, which made me appear unusually solemn as a child and adolescent. Paradoxically, I held on to childhood longer than most of my peers due to my inquisitiveness and being a lifelong tomboy. After all these years, I am still a physically active, curious, and playful child.

I have always been both serious and silly, but during this period of my life, I was often overly serious, focusing on life's distractions. That changed over time as I weathered the ups and downs of life and gained perspective. At some point in adulthood the playful side that my mother nurtured overcame my serious side. The stories shared here bridge that transition.

Nurturing
My Tomboy Nature

Momma and I carried on a "nature versus nurture" argument over the years. She took the "nature" side, claiming I emerged from the womb with my present personality fully intact. I carried the "nurture" baton, believing my environment and my interactions with people formed me. I feared acknowledging the importance of nature meant I couldn't change and would be stuck with an inborn, unalterable fate. Momma never changed her mind, but my understanding evolved.

I began seeing some truth in Momma's stance as I watched my nieces grow from infancy into adulthood. Each niece asserted her personality from birth, and this personhood was nudged by experience as she grew. My early view was too simplistic, and I now understand that we are born with predispositions rather than specific genetic destinies. Today, most experts believe the inseparable forces of "nature" and "nurture" interact in complex and nuanced ways to shape the individual.

From the beginning I was not a girly girl. Momma said when she dressed me in feminine frills and lace, I stripped down to diapers in less than 20 minutes. I still don't care for flouncy garments. As I grew, my preferred activities were running, bicycling, wading in puddles and creeks, and climbing trees. Daddy taught me how to bat, throw, and catch a softball, and pass and receive a football. I abhorred being thought of as a sissy. Doods (rhymes with "goods"), our caretaker, said, "Ruthie, God used a boy pattern to cut you out and then changed His mind and turned you into a girl." This seemed accurate at the time and still does.

I had one doll because I thought all girls should have a doll but didn't play with it. Momma, also not a girly girl, was athletic when she was young and stayed active most of her life. But she was a member of her generation, wearing high heels, skirts, jewelry, and lipstick. I wear minimal makeup and no lipstick, don't like heels or dresses, have never pierced my ears, and wear only rings for jewelry.

Upon entering elementary school in 1958, I declared I wanted to be a boy with the rock-solid argument that boys could wear pants to school while girls had to wear dresses, a social rule enforced in dress codes. I wanted to wear pants like the boys. They were more practical for playing sports, swinging and sliding on playground equipment, and climbing trees. And they were more comfortable than dresses, which were worn with scratchy slips under them.

I played kickball with the boys rather than "house" with the girls and enjoyed fight contests with boys, winning nearly every time. The fights ended in the fifth grade when an older boy who had failed fifth grade twice gripped me in a headlock for what seemed like an eternity. As panic developed, my short life paraded before my eyes. I promised myself to give up fighting if I survived and kept that vow. But I remained active and focused my competitive spirit on sport rivalries. It didn't make me popular, but I was known for being strong and athletic. My reward was verbal: "You do pretty good, *for a girl.*"

I had a small circle of female friends including my best friend. But I always chose to be active and play games when there was an opportunity to do so, and that was always with the boys. At the time, it seemed I didn't fully fit with either group, but in retrospect I was a member of both and learned how to negotiate two playground worlds: I could play by girl-rules or boy-rules. This early exposure gave me tools to navigate gender issues in the work world later in life.

By the teen years, girls were expected to give up rough outdoor play, which didn't make sense. Why should going from age 12 to 13 make such a difference? Nothing had changed to make playing kickball and climbing trees no longer fun. I continued to play games and do outdoor activities rather than traditional indoor girl pursuits. In high school I played pick-up basketball with the guys at church. I can still hear them say, "You do pretty good *for a girl.*" But I didn't care because it was fun, and I could hold my own.

I played junior varsity and varsity basketball and ran track in middle and high school, the only options for young women in the 1960s. I wanted to make a career of it, perhaps as a coach or physical education teacher, but everyone said my interest would pass. They were only partly right—in later years my research career centered around promoting physical activity.

Women were considered too delicate for vigorous activity, but I saw the women in my family work circles around most men. My high school basketball coach said to me in public at practice, "I ain't never seen a girl sweat so much." Maybe most girls my age didn't work as hard as me. My senior year in high school I was voted the senior superlative for "most athletic" at a time when that designation was stigmatizing for women.

In girls track we were permitted three events per meet. I ran the half mile and mile relay and needed another event, preferably without a lot of running. Short distance sprints were out because I was not fast enough to be competitive nor was I a jumper. That left throwing the discus. I taught myself how to do it by reading a book. It was a sight to watch me, discus in one hand and book in the other, spinning around while reading out loud. I eventually learned it well enough to place third in a state meet.

The rules of basketball at that time did not allow girls teams to play full court. During my years in high school, two full court players, called rovers, were allowed, and that was my position. I wanted to be where the action was. The longest event allowed for girls in track was the half-mile as the mile was considered too much for a young lady. It wasn't true, because I routinely ran a mile on my own. Or maybe I wasn't a lady. Many people over the years encouraged me to be more lady-like, from aunts to well-intended strangers.

"Young ladies" behaved in a subdued manner and deferred to males in addition to wearing dresses, makeup, and jewelry, all designed to make one more attractive to members of the opposite sex. I felt smothered with makeup and jewelry, like I was pretending to be someone else, and it got in the way of playing sports. I had been one of the "guys" so far, competing and interacting with them as equals and saw no reason to change now. As a result, none of the boys I went to school with ever asked me on a date nor was I romantically interested in them. My high school boyfriend attended a different school.

Ultimately, the girly rules pointed young women toward "settling down," getting married, and raising a family, preferably after finishing high school. But what if I didn't want to get married after high school or even college? My parent's marriage was a solid partnership, but theirs seemed to be the exception.

Many of my girlfriends' mothers sacrificed personal autonomy to their husbands, which didn't seem like a good deal to me. I understood marriage and motherhood were expected roles of females and proclaimed neither were for me. Everyone said I would change my mind later, but I didn't think so.

I graduated from Walterboro High School in spring 1970. My dream of wearing long pants to school was never realized during twelve years of public education due to unchanging dress codes. I put on a pair of blue jeans when I entered college in fall 1970 and have worn dresses rarely since.

I remained active through college playing intramural sports. There were few options for women at Clemson in the early 70s, but these limitations for young women changed with the passage of Title IX in 1972. It was too late for me, but I am grateful young women now have more opportunities. During college the familiar phrase rang in my ears, "You do pretty good, *for a girl.*" It applied to many of my endeavors, not just the athletic ones, but I didn't let it get to me. Or at least, not much.

My parents gave me a Raleigh Grand Prix bicycle as a graduation gift in May 1974. I loved the bike and rode it many years—the bicycle and my body felt as one. I still have this bicycle, now considered "antique." After college, I also ran and frequently entered competitive 10K road races, about six miles, staying active through my graduate programs.

I began my doctoral degree in 1983 and continued to run, though I stopped competing, and began teaching at the University of Virginia in Charlottesville in August 1986, one week after graduating from my doctoral program. I felt like the same person, still doing pretty good for a girl. I talked proudly with one of my students about the number of miles I ran per week and my other fitness activities. And then she said it: "You do pretty good, *for someone your age.*" I had crossed some imperceptible threshold—a new era had begun.

Aging has not changed my active tomboy nature. In fact, more exercise is needed to maintain the body status quo. I now walk instead of run and added yoga about ten years ago. Shortly after retirement I started swimming laps, and within the past year, I integrated core-strengthening and weight training into my routine. At this rate, exercise will consume my whole day by the age of 100. I embrace being a tomboy until the end.

*   *   *

How did I turn out this way? From a nurture perspective, maybe I wanted to please my father who wanted a boy. My father played football, taught me sport skills, and played ball games with me as though I were a boy, and I loved it. My mother who played basketball in high school supported this. And I was reinforced for being active because I was good at it.

But that also points to the "nature" side. I had two athletic parents and probably inherited genes that predisposed me to being coordinated, active, and enjoying it. I welcomed learning sports from my father because I was already inclined that way. My drive to move and to do things my own way predisposed me to play sporting games with the boys.

"Nature," which predisposed me to be athletic, and "nurture," being raised in an environment where this was modeled and encouraged by those close to me, worked together to shape a tomboy. It was not possible to separate the two sets of influences.

Both Momma and I were partly right in our "nature versus nurture" debate because people are shaped by both. But we were also wrong, because the forces that fashion who we are cannot be considered as separate opposing entities but are a single, interactive process. I did not want to be a boy but did want to wear pants instead of dresses as a practical matter. Gender identity was not an issue for me, and I am boringly straight. I preferred being female and saw that girls had role flexibility, though at the cost of being "popular." I strongly support equality for all humans and do not view my experiences solely as a gender issue. I was simply a child who was determined to be active and play outside. And I wouldn't have had it any other way.

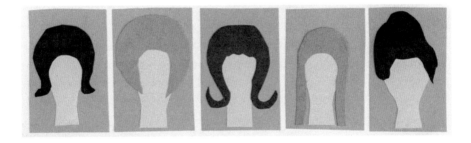

Hair Hypocrisy

I made a deal with my hair in the seventh grade: I wouldn't meddle with it beyond washing, drying, and occasional trims if it would more-or-less behave. This covert negotiation took place around the time I realized I was not destined to be popular, a member of the "in crowd" or admired for my beauty. This frank acceptance of reality at age 12 took a lot of pressure off me and allowed me to focus on athletics and my studies rather than my social life. This was a straightforward decision, because I was painfully reticent in groups.

Still, in the throes of the middle school years, it seemed important to maintain some standards of appearance to forestall further declines in social status. Hours of preadolescent scrutiny in the bathroom mirror fixed on two flaws: my nose, which was too big, and my hair, which laid flat on my head except for the cowlick on the right side causing my bangs to flip up. Cosmetic surgery for the nose was out of my reach, so I concentrated on the hair.

The fashionable hair styles of the mid-1960s featured fullness on the top, tapering as the hair reached the bottom of the ear, curving into a uniform upward flip around the bottom, especially for longer hair. For shorter hairstyles, the fullness on top was augmented by teasing, sometimes producing the classic "beehive" do. My hair refused to cooperate with curlers to create the upward flip and teasing created something more akin to a tangled rats' nest than a smooth beehive. Taming the cowlick was futile—the bangs wouldn't cover it, and no matter where I parted my hair, it always reverted to the right side. That's when I called the truce, stopped fighting with my hair, and let it be.

My earlier hair history was uneventful with a few notable incidences. The first was in the third grade when my mother took my sister and me to a beautician who decided that our middle length hair would be more attractive cut short. She chopped it off. My sister and I cried for hours. At school the next day one of our classmates, a young boy known for being outspoken, proclaimed we had been bushwhacked. We felt humiliated. After this experience, Momma gave us complete control of our hair. We let it grow.

The next hair episode occurred in the fifth grade. My mid-length hair hung straight, a low maintenance hairstyle that suited my personality. My Aunt determined I was old enough to put some effort into attracting the attention of boys. Surely some curls would add to my sex appeal. She undertook lost causes on my behalf throughout my childhood, mostly aimed at increasing my femininity.

The path she chose to change my straight flat hair into sexy curls was a permanent wave. She ran me down and carried me kicking and screaming to her kitchen sink where she proceeded with the promised hair treatment. It smelled terrible, but I've blanked out other details of the experience. She liked the results, but I did not. My hair, tightly wound into curls, bounced as I moved about, as though I had someone else's hair on my head. I resolved there would be no more perms or curls for me! According to my mother, I was born to be a plain person, at least in appearance. I was the firstborn, and being a girl, Momma fancied dressing me up in frills and lace, like a doll baby. It wasn't meant to be. She couldn't do curls because I had no hair for the first two years of my life.

My hair grew long in high school, reaching down my back by the college years. This worked out well, as it complemented my hippie look along with the blue jeans and t-shirts. Simple and low maintenance. I didn't cut my hair until I'd been out of college and started working, but I kept my promise of no perms, curlers, or hot irons. And it kept its end of the bargain and behaved. It sometimes flipped out in a wayward direction on the right side, but that's probably related to that cowlick. Just let it be.

In my late 20s, I went back on the promise to my hair one time. I had it permed and regretted it. It probably looked fine but did not feel right. It also damaged my hair, causing it to dry out and be unmanageable for months—probably revenge for my transgression.

In the decades since I have left my hair alone other than basic washing, drying, and an occasional trim. I should say *mostly* left it alone. In my early 30s I started "touching up" the premature gray that appeared. Early graying is common in women on my mother's side of the family and all of them colored their hair. I remember Momma walking around the house with dark goo in her hair on color days. Her mother entered the nursing home in her 80s with brown hair. I accepted hair color as a fact of life.

As time progressed, touching up the gray became applying full hair color at home. When that could no longer cover the encroaching white, I had it professionally done. In the beginning I justified going back on my promise because I was "prematurely gray." At some point in the now distant past the white hair was no longer premature, and I had no excuse. But, following the family tradition, I continue to do it. My hair was not happy when I colored at home, but it accepts the professional treatments with no complaints.

Hair typically turns gray and then white as people age in a process known as *achromotrichia*. The age graying starts is due mostly to genetics, but the environment can also influence this process. Changes in hair color occur when the hair root no longer produces melanin and new hairs grow in without pigment.

I am considering the next big step in my hair care journey and returning fully to the promise I made to my hair in the seventh grade: to let it grow out and be itself. I try to imagine myself with a white head of hair, but it is difficult. I thought I would let it return to its natural state when I retired. At retirement, I told myself the time would be right when I turned 70. As I get closer to 70, 75 seems more reasonable for such a dramatic transition. Or perhaps 80—or maybe when I enter a nursing home.

My hair has kept up its end of the bargain much better than I have. But I am working on overcoming my hair hypocrisy.

Learning on the Job

During high school summers I began learning about what kind of work I liked by working in jobs that had a lot of things I did not like. It was like having to create puzzle pieces before being able to piece them together. At first, I thought being able to do the required tasks was the only thing that mattered. Through experience, I found other pieces of the puzzle: the physical setting, the social environment, and liking or finding meaning in the work tasks. I began creating and assembling these elements in my high school summer employment as a tobacco farm worker, legal secretary's assistant, and camp counselor.

*   *   *

My first job outside of doing chores at home was summer work as a tobacco worker on a farm belonging to the father of a close friend. Earning money by doing hard labor was rewarding; I am my father's daughter, after all. Working under the hot sun with bugs was manageable because we also had fun.

Tobacco work changed as the tobacco plants developed. We started with "topping and suckering" young plants by detaching the flowering top and removing small green shoots, also known as suckers, growing between the stalk and leaves. The work was unpleasant: thick, sticky juice from the plant covered you head to toe. After the morning and afternoon sessions we changed into bathing suits and headed for the pond on the family property with a bar of soap to scrub off the gunk. It didn't take long to wash, and we lingered in the pond enjoying ourselves.

The next phase started when tobacco leaves began to ripen. Leaves lower on the plant were ready first; those higher ripened later. The large, yellowish leaves were picked by hand or cropped and attached in clusters by stringing them onto long sturdy sticks. I was a stringer, and our work crew had the advantage of the latest machinery for cropping and stringing. A tractor slowly pulled an apparatus with adjustable seats for four pairs of workers through the rows of plants, enabling cropping and stringing to take place together. The cropper, who sat lower on the apparatus, removed leaves from the plant and passed them to the stringer above, who attached them to the stick as they were received. A ninth person removed and stacked sticks of tobacco and would troubleshoot problems. The process required skill and choreography among the nine workers. I don't know how something so complicated worked in a hot field.

I was a good stringer and loved the rhythmic movement and group coordination as though we formed a single machine. The repetitive motion of stringing caused a minor but persistent overuse injury in my upper back which still flares up when I'm tired. I didn't complain, because I valued doing my part for the work crew, and at the end of the week, we got paid $10 a day in cash. In the mid-1960s this seemed like a small fortune.

The sticks of green tobacco were hung in heated barns to dry. When the first barn was cured, my friend and I moved to the dry tobacco process. We transferred the sticks to a shed and spread special sheets on the ground. We removed the leaves from the sticks and sorted or graded them onto different sheets based on quality, determined by the presence and amount of mold, leaf deterioration, and contaminants. The full sheets were bundled by folding and tying opposite corners into knots. Nearly all of it went to market, regardless of condition.

The hours were long, starting shortly after sunrise through late into the day. But we took a two-hour lunch break when it was hottest. I shared a midday meal with the family, and we watched the soaps after eating. This was the only time in my life I became addicted to daytime TV. Each day I looked forward to the next installment of betrayals, affairs, crises, and comas. Working in the field was physically challenging, but in most ways, this was a fun job, because I worked among friends, and I was good at it.

The 1960s were a different time. Public smoking was the norm, and concerns about tobacco use as a health hazard were new. My career in public health and widespread acceptance of the dangers of tobacco were a distant and unforeseen future. Perhaps this job nudged me toward public health. It certainly sealed my aversion to the use of tobacco. Most of the bugs fell off the tobacco leaves during the curing process, but some went to market, as did the leaves with mold and rot. I could never smoke knowing what went into the product.

*   *   *

The setting of my next summer job was an improvement over being outside in the hot sun and in contact with toxic plants and bugs. My mother was a professional legal secretary, so I had an inside track on temporary positions as a legal secretary's assistant. I was paid minimum wage, $2.76 per hour, which I thought was good money. I answered the phone, took messages, filed, and did simple typing.

One task was to type separate copies of a form letter to 300 different people. They had to be originals, so no carbon paper was allowed; this was before copy machines and word processing had been invented. I dutifully banged out 300 perfect letters on a manual typewriter. I typed far more than 300, because I had to start over when I made a mistake. Then the lawyer proofread his draft and found a less-than-optimal word. I couldn't believe I had to redo all the letters. My mother pointed out I had to be doing something, and it didn't matter what it was, so it might just as well be typing those letters. This sage observation did not help. But it was an early lesson in coping with impatience and my desire for quick closure, something I grapple with today.

I had a similar experience typing simple Wills. No corrections were allowed because the Will could be contested. I did get a few completed, but only after many tries and much frustration. I was more capable of answering the phone, but dreaded it because I was timid which made talking to strangers difficult. I was also able to do the filing but found it boring and lived in fear of misfiling an important document.

I looked forward to walking deposits to the bank, because this removed me from the office. The air-conditioned law office setting had clear advantages over working under the hot sun, but I found legal work to be dull. I was not good at being a secretary's assistant in part because I wasn't good at this work and found the setting and law practice unappealing. I learned two essential lessons from this work: I didn't want to work as a secretary, nor did I want to be a lawyer.

*   *   *

My last summer job in high school took me from a law office to a pine forest. I worked as a counselor at Camp Millcreek for six weeks. It served physically handicapped children who were not eligible for other camps. Its sister site, Camp Burnt Gin, is still in operation. At Millcreek, I loved working with the children. But interacting with people of different ranks within the organization was challenging, and the physical environment was harsh.

Our primary focus as counselors were the children; we supervised them 24/7. We kept them clean, ensured they attended meals and activities, and got them to bed at night. We also did the housekeeping. I enjoyed arts and crafts and swimming, which provided welcome respite from the stifling heat of the pine woods. Campers addressed counselors by a respectful title, "Miss" or "Mr.," plus first name; children and adults called me "Miss Ruthie."

I don't remember what we got paid. We were on duty 24 hours, so the hourly wage probably amounted to a few cents per hour. But one does not do this for the money. Many of the children were shunned by peers and adults. One little boy had an eye deformity; some counselors could not make eye contact or express affection toward him. The pain of repeated rejection permeated his being, and I resolved to accept and love him as he was.

Some campers came from impoverished backgrounds and had parents or guardians who were overwhelmed. One camper showed up on the bus for multiple camping sessions each summer because he had nowhere else to go; no adults from his hometown noticed he was gone. I stayed in touch with some of my campers as pen pals for years. I received one letter with only the address: "mis Ruthe, Wlturbuh, SC." Our mail carrier was familiar with the families on his rural route and knew where to deliver the letter, but I have no idea how it made it to the Walterboro post office.

One camp-out night was required in each session. One group of my young campers thought eating outside, roasting marshmallows by campfire, and singing under the stars were great fun. They were stunned with dismay and disbelief when they realized they were also going to sleep outside in tents. I felt the same way; I simply cannot sleep on the ground.

The routine accommodations were only slightly better than camping out. The counselors slept in bunk beds on screened porches attached to the rustic cabins in which the campers stayed. It was hot and stuffy with a lot of mosquitoes. I had a toxic reaction to excessive bites and was surprised my supervisor was annoyed with me, as though I were to blame for the problem.

This was my first job with people who were not relatives or friends. There were many employees in a strict hierarchy; entry level counselors like me were on the lowest rung of the organization. At the time, it seemed I irritated those above me. Even the way I swept the floor was criticized, and I could not understand why. In retrospect, I did not know how to navigate the camp bureaucracy and probably failed to show the appropriate respect for authority and procedures. The work with the children was meaningful, and I liked contributing to the better good. But the working environment was not supportive and distracted me from the important tasks related to the children. I learned the about the importance of knowing "how things are done" in the organization.

*   *   *

I was fortunate to have an assortment of summer jobs in high school. I earned spending money and saved for the future. No single summer job was ideal because I needed all puzzle pieces: able to do the work, liking or finding meaning in the tasks, feeling supported socially, and working in a personally compatible physical environment. As an adult I assembled the puzzle pieces during 30 years in an academic setting. I preferred working a clean and quiet indoor environment with people, ideas, and numbers, and I thrived in supportive and collegial settings. But what got me through rough spots as a working adult was knowing that *I can do almost anything—for three months.*

Mrs. Roth

I lived in an apartment on North Main when I moved to Columbia, South Carolina in 1976. It was a time of change following graduate school, when I was searching for "what I wanted to be when I grow up." At age 24 I did not have a driver's license, much less a car. The apartment was affordable and convenient to a bus line downtown, where I worked. I had some rather odd neighbors, or so it seemed at the time. But I formed a lasting friendship with one of them—an older lady named Mrs. Roth.

Mrs. Roth lived alone. Her daughter and son-in-law lived locally but rarely visited, and she wanted company. I had no roommate, a new job I didn't like, and few connections. We were an odd couple, separated in age by around five decades, but united in our isolation. Our apartments were adjacent, and I visited her several times a week. After about a year, we both moved from the North Main apartments. I went to Forest Acres, and she went to the Irmo area to live near her daughter. I'd gotten my driver's license and a car in the meantime, so I continued to visit her about once per week for nearly eight years.

At first, our conversations were somewhat one-sided; she talked, and I listened and had trouble getting any words in. I finally realized she couldn't hear me and was too proud to acknowledge it. I sat closer to her and spoke slowly and distinctly. But she could always outtalk me. Four decades later I recall the times we spent together with fondness.

Mrs. Roth was born in Germany and immigrated to western New York with her parents when she was small. She became a proud and loyal US citizen. Her deceased husband was a baker. She was somewhat short and stout, with closely cropped, completely white hair. She referred to herself frequently as a "red-headed girl" and talked about things "the old folks" said. This always amused me because her hair was clearly not red and to my youthful thinking, she *was* one of the "old folks."

Mrs. Roth loved plants and kept many in her apartment. She gave me a single stem-and-leaf cutting from her peace lily early in our relationship. From this small beginning the plant grew and survived pot transplants and many moves. It even outlasted a series of three cats. Willie was not interested in the plant, but he excavated dirt from the pot—for the joy of digging as he did not leave "fertilizer" behind. Tinkerbell nibbled the greenery, and Miss Noki chowed down on it before I rescued it. It thrives today, 40-plus years after she gave me the cutting. It blooms frequently with white flowers. I think of Mrs. Roth and her white hair every time I see it.

In her final years, Mrs. Roth's health declined. She lost her vision and suffered from increasing pain. I knew she wasn't doing well but was shocked and saddened when she passed away in 1983 while I was out of town. I learned with dismay about her death and cremation in a single phone conversation with her daughter. I needed to see her one more time than was possible.

At her memorial service, I expected my behavior to be quiet and dignified and brought only one tissue. I missed my friend, but her health and quality of life had suffered; she was at rest now. And I was calm when the service started. But then the minister began telling stories about Mrs. Roth's remarkable ability to cope with increasing adversity, especially the loss of her vision. He described how she folded clothes, matched socks, and poured her own drinks without overflowing the glass. Tears streamed down my face, but it didn't stop there. I bawled and sobbed with deep gasps for breath for the remainder of the service. I was so embarrassed and was the only person expressing grief so vocally. Some kind person passed handfuls of tissues to help me cope with the floods.

I remained ill at ease about her death and distracted for some time after the memorial service. There was guilt for not being there at the end and anger over the cremation which deprived me of a final visit. Her death happened at the start of a new phase of my life, when I was entering graduate school to make a career shift that I wasn't comfortable with yet. I felt frustrated starting something new before I had closure on an important part of my old life. Months went by with few opportunities to resolve the grief, guilt, and anger.

One night, I dreamed about Mrs. Roth. We were standing on an open deck on a clear night, something we never did when she was alive. It was evident she had died and come back to visit me. I said, "I miss you" and didn't know what to say next. There was a long silence as we stood together in the night. My eyes found the dark sky, filled with bright stars. I commented, "The stars are very beautiful." She looked at me and said, "Yes, and I am much closer to them now." I realized that Mrs. Roth was gone but that our relationship remained.

Instantly the weight of my guilt and anger lifted, and my uneasiness over her passing dissipated into the calm evening. I awoke from the dream, grateful for her comforting visit and friendship, transcending even death.

Driven to Distraction

I relied on my bicycle and friends and family for my limited transportation needs when I was in high school, college, and graduate school in the 1960s and early 1970s. But I found a different world when in 1976 I moved to Columbia, SC to work at age 24. The bicycle was not feasible or safe for the six-mile commute to work in heavy traffic. I used the city bus, but the timing and stops were inconvenient. I felt forced to revisit my declaration made at age 14: "I will never learn to drive!"

There was a good reason for such a declaration in 1966. Driving lessons in my family consisted of the trainee driving the family two miles to and from Sunday church services on a rural highway. It was an efficient use of time. We always went to church, so two adults were available to supervise, the car was available, and the route was mapped out. But getting a family of five with children aged 14, 12, and 8 years fed, dressed in Sunday-best, and in the car to arrive on time for 10:00 am Sunday School was challenging and stressful enough without the added burden of group instruction. I thought it was ironic that getting ready to go to church resulted in family members exhibiting higher-than-usual levels of unholy behavior. And that was before the morning of my driving-lesson-in-the-family-car-going-to-church crucible.

On that warm Sunday morning, I sat self-consciously behind the wheel. Daddy was in the passenger seat, and Momma was in the back with my brother and sister. Before the car was in motion, Daddy and Momma braced their bodies as though they were preparing for the impact of an imminent crash. My sister and brother were more relaxed and looking forward to some entertainment at the expense of their older sister on the way to church. I took a deep breath.

Every step of the process was a big deal to me. Where do I put the key? How far should I turn it? How hard should I turn it? Where do I put my feet? How do I change the gear to move in reverse? How do I hold my head when I am backing up? How many times do I have to look both directions before I turn onto the road? I kept these frantic deliberations to myself. After what seemed like an eternity, I started the car, backed to turn around in the driveway, and headed onto the road. A chorus of shouts spontaneously arose.

With rising pitch and sense of annoyance Daddy exclaimed, "Turn if you are going to turn. Get on the road!" A sibling echoed, "Yeah, don't go so slow!"

I speeded up.

Momma pleaded, "Not so fast. Slow down!" A sibling repeated, "Yeah, slow down!"

I slowed down.

Momma: "Not that slow—you have to drive." A sibling restated, "Yeah, go faster!"

I speeded up.

Daddy, with irritation in his voice, "Don't jerk the car! Just drive it smooth."

I slowed down.

Momma shouted, "No, not like that!" Siblings called out unison, "Can I drive instead? Daddy, speaking on top of my siblings, continued with urgency and exasperation, "No, no, that's not how you do it! You need to…. Watch out behind you!"

We had advanced less than 100 yards from the driveway. My pulse and thoughts were racing, and I couldn't breathe. There was no way I could take two miles of this. After the vehicle behind us passed at 60 miles per hour, I pulled over onto the shoulder and declared, "I am not going to learn to drive." I opened the car door and got out of the driver's seat. There were feeble pleas for me to continue, but all were relieved that the lesson was cut short. We shuffled places and continued the short trip to church. I stuck with my pronouncement.

That is, I stubbornly held to it until I moved to Columbia in 1976. I signed up for lessons with a private company I found in the Yellow Pages of the phone book. I couldn't believe it the first time the instructor pulled into to my apartment parking lot, slid to the passenger seat and patted the driver's seat for me to get in. Her only words were, "You drive."

I had hoped to observe for a few weeks before getting behind the wheel. I balked, but she insisted. I was nervous but relieved to see that the instructor had steering and break controls on her side of the vehicle. We headed downtown into Columbia's morning rush-hour traffic.

Early on, I almost made a left turn into on-coming traffic on the wrong side of Assembly Street. The instructor quickly took over and guided the car to the correct lane. I was freaking out but had to keep driving. She matter-of-factly explained to me, "All people who learn to drive later in life have something to overcome. For you it is your nerves." I dreaded the sessions but gradually gained skills and confidence.

Still, I was apprehensive when it was time to take the driving test. My instructor took me to the highway department. I did well on the written and road tests. But I bumped the post in the parallel parking. The examiner drawled, "Lady, you just hit a brand-new Cadillac." I knew I was not going to pass but held the tears until I was back inside with my instructor. I did well in school and was unaccustomed to failing tests.

I waited the required two weeks and returned with my instructor to the highway department for another test. When she saw the assigned examiner, she whispered to me, "Drive very slowly, and you will pass." Obediently, in the road test I drove 5 miles below the speed limit of 30. The examiner braced in his seat and exclaimed, "Slow down!" I slowed down to 20 miles per hour and passed the road as well as the parallel parking tests with no problems. I obtained my driver's license at age 24. Daddy and Momma gave me a 1976 red Dodge Dart as a gift. I was elated.

The Dart was memorable. It tended to slide when the brakes were applied, especially on wet pavement. Shortly after I got it, I was in a car accident in rain and heavy rush-hour traffic going home from work. I applied the brakes to avoid hitting the car in front of me, skidded and scratched the side of a brand-new Cadillac in the next lane. I considered the possibility that the first driving test examiner had been a prophet. Fortunately, no one was injured. I was charged with driving too fast for conditions and was distraught. I am grateful to the law enforcement officer who sat with me in the rain until I had settled down enough to drive to my apartment, long after the paperwork was done.

I was visibly anxious when I appeared at traffic court. Neither the officer on the scene or the other driver showed up. The presiding judge noted my emotional state and provided subtle but clear guidance, "GIVEN that the officer is not present, and GIVEN that the plaintiff is not present, how do you plead?" I managed to squeak out a timid, "Not guilty?" My insurance had paid for the damage to the other car, and there were no fines or points lost. And that was that.

Later in its automotive life, the Dart developed an appetite for consuming alternators. It was so bad the repair shop stopped charging me for them. My theory was that my stress levels were so high it shorted out the electrical system in my car. After 10 years of buying a new car one part at a time, I knew it was time to replace the Dart all at once with a new vehicle.

I don't enjoy shopping for a new car, and it was the hardest for the first. I don't know why I grew so attached to the Dart, because it let me down on the highway and in the parking lot repeatedly. I prepared myself emotionally for a lengthy grieving process. At the car dealer, I test drove a light blue Mustang and liked it—it was a lot zoomier than the Dart, and it didn't skid. I never looked back as I left the parking lot in the new car.

I find some routines to be comforting, making life more predictable and less stressful. Getting the "lesson" in 1966, the Dart in 1976, and the Mustang in 1986 established a comforting rhythm for dealing with cars. I now aim to buy a new car once every ten years whether I need it or not. Car number three was a turquoise 1996 Chevrolet Cavalier. It seemed to have an invisible "kick me" sign on the rear bumper, because I was rear-ended several times in it. I suffered no injuries, but the car was never the same.

Number four was a dark gray 2006 Toyota Matrix I owned for 12 years, the only exception to the 10-year rule. I still miss it, and may never forgive Toyota for no longer manufacturing that model. My current vehicle, number five, is a gray 2018 Ford Escape and the only one I've named. She is called Blue Bell, due to glowing blue dashboard lights and constant reminder dings. Our relationship is in its early stages, and we have until 2028 to work things out.

I've come a long way since 1966. My "nerves" have not been a problem for my driving since the early days. I am thankful to my driving instructor for her calm perseverance during those times, helping me learn to be more focused and less distracted and anxious when driving. I am also grateful for a driver's license and the privilege of automobile ownership, which has enabled me to live and get to work conveniently in Columbia and spend time in Walterboro and Orangeburg with family, especially in my parents' final years.

Matrimony

I never dated anyone in my class, probably a legacy of my tomboy nature. But my high school boyfriend went to a school out of town and visited his grandmother on weekends. We both attended Drs. Creek Baptist Church and had many fun times going to church social events and to concerts in Charleston. Sometimes on Sunday afternoons we went horseback riding with his cousin.

We did not go to dances, and I had no intention of going to my high school prom. But my boyfriend persuaded me to go to the senior prom at his school. When I got there, I refused to dance, because I had never learned how and was too bashful to try in a large crowd of strangers. This hurt his feelings and offended several others who took my refusal as an affront. I was uncomfortable and felt trapped but also guilty about letting my boyfriend and his friends down. The relationship did not last much longer.

When I entered Clemson University in the fall of 1970, the ratio of males to females was 4 to 1. Getting dates was easy but finding one that didn't require advanced skills in self-defense was another matter. I found a great guy and dated him for three years. We had wonderful times together going to movies, concerts, listening to music, and spending time with family. We became engaged to marry after about two years together.

These were years of bewildering and rapid social change and unrest in the country with hippies, drugs, anti-war demonstrations, and civil rights activism. During my freshman year, there was a house mother, we signed in and out of the dormitory, and had a 10 pm weekend curfew. By my senior year, there were equal numbers of males and females, co-ed dorms, and no curfews, signing in or out, or house mothers. I was grateful that things were calm at Clemson in those years.

My boyfriend took part in the most exciting thing that happened: the streaking craze. It was great fun to watch this mostly male spectacle—guys would suddenly abandon what they were doing, rip off their clothes, and join the crowd of naked men running by. But we curious onlookers were disappointed, because the bodies were moving too fast for any meaningful revelation.

The social climate of the country wasn't the only thing that changed during those years. As graduation approached, it became apparent that my boyfriend and I had grown apart. I envisioned graduate school while my fiancée pictured a stay-at-home mom. We amicably ended the engagement, which was difficult for everyone as we had become part of each other's family.

After college came several jobs and bouts of graduate school. I dated, but there were no serious relationships, mainly because I wasn't interested. In 1986, I was in my mid-thirties, finished with years of education, employed in a full-time position, and happily single. All my life I moved of my own accord prompting my mother to comment, "You're always swimming upstream, Ruthie." Always observant, Momma saw and accepted me as I was, even if that meant no grandchildren. She often said, "I am not raising you for me—I am raising you to be on your own." My parents had accepted I was not the marrying type.

So, Momma and Daddy didn't know how to react when, one year into university teaching, I announced my upcoming wedding. My father's first response was, "Are you SURE?" My mother had initial doubts, as well, and watched us closely. At some point she laughed and said with relief, "Well, you both are weird, but your weirdness fits together in a way that makes you compatible." Eleven days short of my 36th birthday in late 1987 I married my husband.

The wedding was small, informal, and short—about eight minutes. It would have been shorter, but the minister threw in a 3-minute prayer. It was almost too long for me. I fell into a longstanding nervous habit in times of stress—holding my breath throughout the ceremony. This was soon followed by lightheadedness and buckling knees. I thought, "Oh, no—I'm going to be a fainting bride!" My alert husband-to-be got my attention and modeled a deep breath. I took a quick breath and managed enough choppy inhales and exhales to prevent a dramatic scene at the altar. We just celebrated 32 years of marriage. The honeymoon is ongoing.

"We're all a little weird, and life's a little weird. And when we find someone whose weirdness is compatible with ours, we join up with them and fall in mutual weirdness and call it love."

— Dr. Seuss

Friskers and Rachel

Friskers and Rachel shared their happy lives with me and my husband for 16 years after a dubious beginning: they were a special mixed breed known as "ditch dogs," so named because that's where the puppies were found in 1991. They were not our first choice for pets. About one week earlier we had adopted two striking, sandy-colored lab-mixes from a litter born near Red Bank, but they disappeared from our fenced-in backyard after a few days. The blond labs were friendly and had a sweetly muffled bark. They looked like nicer specimens than the mutts they were, and we speculated someone took them. We were sad to lose them and posted flyers around our Pine Ridge neighborhood with the futile hope someone would return them to us.

We did get one call. Someone had found two small puppies, likely littermates, in a shoebox placed in the ditch beside Fish Hatchery Road. We were pretty sure these weren't the blond, snuffling, half-grown canines who disappeared from our backyard but went to look at them anyway. We saw two small, young, and dark-colored pups. One had a lot of terrier in her, and the other looked like a lab-mix. We were disappointed, even though we knew ahead of time these were unlikely to be our lost dogs. We returned home. But in that brief time the abandoned sisters had captured our hearts, and we went back to get them.

The dark brown, terrier-like puppy was frisky and had whiskers, so we named her Friskers. She grew up to be skittish. If a car were coming down the road her fear would compel her to run out and roll over in front of it. This submissive behavior might have been adaptive for coping with an aggressive dog but was an unfortunate strategy for handling automobiles. We kept her far away from traffic. The calmer, black pup became Rachel, named after a friend's cat. Rachel had a lab body on short legs and in certain poses looked like a baby seal. She grew up to be Friskers' rock. The two were always together, except for a couple of times when one went to the vet alone. They behaved as two parts of one creature. Friskers was the superego, she always felt guilty about something, and Rachel was the id, she enjoyed everything and everybody. They lacked an ego and shared slightly less than a complete brain between the two. But it didn't matter, because it wasn't needed. They lived in our backyard, and we took care of them.

After they arrived via shoebox, we set up a puppy nursery in the basement. It was immediately clear they were sick. The first night we took them to an emergency clinic; they were infested with worms and required treatment. It was expensive, but it could have been worse; the technician was sympathetic and gave us a two-for-one price because we had adopted strays. I am happy to say they were healthy for the next 16 years.

My husband's father built a doghouse as a "welcome home." They seemed baffled by it, so he crawled inside to show how to use it. They followed him in and enjoyed their backyard home from then on. We brought their small abode with us when we moved to Columbia in 2000.

There were occasional doggie adventures. Like barking all night at an empty aluminum pie plate lodged against the fence by the wind. And sometimes they encountered wild creatures that ventured into our semi-rural Pine Ridge yard.

They mauled a baby opossum one evening, which we rescued and took to the wildlife clinic for recovery. A friend later joked about saving the possum so it could fulfil its destiny as future roadkill. A disoriented, large snapping turtle wandered into the yard one day. Rachel investigated, and she received a bite on the nose and a lifelong scar.

In a nighttime scenario repeated many times, Rachel dug out under the fence while Friskers stayed inside. This was followed by separation anxiety and uncontrollable barking. My husband got out of bed and put Rachel in the yard after blocking the escape hole. And she was out again by the time he returned to bed. Frantic barking resumed. And on it went.

In 2007, after many happy times and escapades, it was time for our pups to move on. Rachel died first with a tumor. We worried about Friskers, fearing she would be lost without her lifelong guardian and companion. But a curious thing happened in those final months. About the time Rachel got sick, a white cat showed up in the backyard, apparently to hang out with the elderly siblings. Rachel couldn't see or hear well and took little notice of the cat, but Friskers liked the visitor. We thought it had been raised around dogs, became displaced, and needed canine company. I started feeding the kitty. After Rachel died, the cat became Friskers' constant companion, easing her grief. It was quite a sight watching them greet nose-to-nose and walk side-by-side; we were grateful for Friskers' feline friend arriving at such an opportune time.

Friskers died from kidney failure a few months later. We were sad and missed our pups, but I looked forward to getting to know the new cat better; small consolation is better than none. But it was not meant to be. She was gone by the time we returned home on the day we lost Friskers. We never saw the white cat again. It compounded my grief until I understood. We call her the "Angel Cat," because she alleviated Friskers' grief and loneliness in her final months. She taught me to remain open to unexpected moments of comfort, especially when I am distracted by grief.

Why a cat would seek out and become a companion to dying creatures is one of life's delightful mysteries. Perhaps the Angel Cat was an emissary from beyond, sent to escort Rachel and Friskers to the next life. After all, they were good dogs.

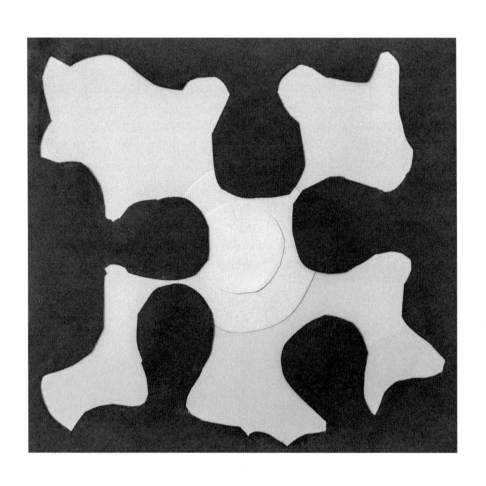

Surgery

Emergency exploratory surgery is not a pleasant way to start your day. But I didn't have much choice on Thursday, May 13, 1999. Years later, I reflect on how the day which could have been my last was a new beginning.

The Wednesday before had been an ordinary day for a university professor: a long meeting in the morning and teaching class all afternoon. I was deeply distressed because of the issues brought up at the meeting. Ironically, the class was stress management. But, I thought, maybe talking about handling pressure and practicing relaxation was a great follow-on to a difficult morning. I just had to ignore the nagging stomachache.

The class topic was perfect for me: an examination of one's priorities in life, a discussion about how urgency is not the same as importance, a perspective-building activity, and relaxation practice. For the activity, I explained how the uncomfortable experience of imagining yourself witnessing your own funeral provides valuable insight about what is important. I demonstrated with a personal scenario: I saw myself at my funeral with family and friends gathered around, talking about me and my life. And not one of them said, "What a pity, she could have published so many more papers!" The class laughed.

I felt good about the class and looked forward to meeting with the students the next day. I met my husband at a restaurant on the way home for supper, even though the stomachache worsened. After I'd eaten, I felt unwell. When I got home, I lay down on the sofa; I was sure resting there would help.

It did not. I tried to go to bed but was miserable and up by midnight. I knew this was not a stress-related symptom and being able to teach class the following day was becoming less likely. My husband was up with me several times. I left the bedroom, closed the bedroom door, and returned to the sofa. I saw no point in disturbing his sleep because I was having a bad time.

My condition worsened. I was in more pain than words can describe and passed out while lying on the sofa. I knew this was serious. I wanted to tell my husband but could not get up on my own or speak loudly enough for him to hear me. I bumped on the floor with my foot until I got his attention. To this day I fear he is haunted by the sound of my bumping in the night.

We called our family doctor's answering service around 4:00 am. The physician on call phoned us back. My husband described the symptoms of pain and passing out. The physician said fainting could be due to pain and it would be probably be safe to wait until the morning. So, we remained at home.

My situation deteriorated further. I moved in and out of consciousness, mostly out. When I started gasping for breath, my husband called his parents to help get me to the hospital. I recognized my life was in danger.

I considered the possibility I would die, leaving behind the people I loved and accepted this possibility completely. The prior weekend had been Mother's Day, and we had good, separate visits with both mothers, good final memories. If it were my time to go, then I would go, and it would be OK. If it were not my time to go, then I was in good hands, and things would be fine. At that moment I experienced a sense of peace greater than the intensity of the abdominal pain, which was considerable. My awareness of the outside world fluctuated from moment to moment, but my inner world was alive.

Looking back, my sense of calm was probably caused by low oxygen levels in the brain. I am grateful for this quirk of physiology. A week after this incident was successfully resolved, with brain fully oxygenated, I was terrified to consider how close to death I came; I did not want to leave my loved ones, especially my husband.

My in-laws arrived. My father-in-law single-handedly carried me from the living room sofa to his car. I am not lightweight; transporting my mostly unconscious form was like carrying an oddly shaped sack of lead drawn toward the earth by a greater-than-usual gravitational force. But when he set his mind to something, it got done. In moments of consciousness on the trip to the hospital I mentally noted how soft and comfortable the seat in my in-law's car felt.

I remembered reaching Lexington Medical Center emergency room, which is remarkable, because I later learned my blood pressure of 40/0 upon arrival indicated I was barely alive. Things happened quickly and much of it was a blur. I was lying on a stretcher; a lot of people leaned over, peering at me and probing as they ticked through a list of medical considerations. It reminded me of a hospital emergency TV show with me playing the starring role. Except I was not playing—this was for real. I felt well-tended and remained calm.

I was aware the medical staff didn't understand the problem. I was losing blood internally, but the origin of the bleeding was undetermined. They started fluid and blood infusions as they were trying to figure it out. I thought, "I sure hope they have screened the blood." In a moment of clarity, I realized the blood was necessary to my immediate survival; concerns about blood contamination would have to wait or there would be no later time.

The staff conducted unrevealing tests. One of them was a memorable nose-to-stomach tube to check gastric contents. I screamed throughout this procedure, because participating in this way helped me cope with the discomfort. It did not benefit anyone within earshot. The final test was a CT scan. I remember it because I had to sit up, which was difficult as well as painful.

A doctor with the bluest blue eyes I'd ever seen leaned inches away from my face, looking directly into my eyes as he spoke. He explained, "The CT scan revealed a large mass of an unknown nature in your lower abdomen. We need to do emergency exploratory surgery to identify and deal with the problem." The medical staff, all the way through the anesthetist, explained every detail as they prepared me. I felt I was in capable hands and appreciated how they described everything to me, without knowing if I understood what they were saying. And I looked forward to the surgery. I had to have some relief from the pain—one way or the other and sooner rather than later.

I awoke in the recovery room and became aware of masses of tubes connected to my body. The one which immediately captured complete attention was the ventilator. It was not scary or painful, but it was annoying because it breathed for me; I wanted control of my breathing. But it was evident the machine had the upper hand; I acceded to it. It is frightening to see a loved one inundated with tubes connected to medical equipment, but my experience of this episode compared to that of family members was not bad. After all, I was alive and fully conscious. Invasive medical intervention turned out to be a temporary, life-saving measure for which I remain thankful.

I could not talk with a tube down my windpipe, so someone held a small whiteboard and gave me a marker. I scribbled a question to my husband, "What happened?" He explained the internal bleeding and straightforward surgical repair, concluding with "Everything will be OK." I thought, "Good—I knew it would work out." My next written question was, "How long?" He thought I meant how much time had elapsed, but I shook my head and pointed to the tube down my throat; I wanted to know how long I was going to be on the ventilator. He replied, "The doctor said it would be several days." I wrote: "Too long." Fortunately for me, I recovered enough for it to be removed later the same day.

The medical name for this uncommon condition—internal bleeding from an abdominal artery—is *abdominal apoplexy*. An artery on my large intestine had "sprung a leak" and was bleeding out into my body cavity. The abdominal mass on the CT scan was a pool of blood and the pain was caused by the accumulating fluid displacing body organs. It was a simple fix once the doctors saw it from the inside and is a common traumatic injury, such as a car crash injury. Except I had experienced no trauma. I asked the surgeon if stress triggered it; he said, "Definitely not. People would be dropping on the street." The cause was a mystery.

I was transferred to the intensive care unit (ICU) after surgery; I called it the intensive *glare* unit—they never turned off the lights. It might be the most uncomfortable place in the hospital—but they don't want you to be comfortable, they want you to stay alive. I was supposed to be there for a week and possibly in the hospital longer. But I was out of the ICU within one day and out of the hospital two days later.

The surgeon later said, "Not many people come back from where you were," and attributed my rapid recovery to a high level of health and fitness before the incident. I always thought being fit and healthy might prevent a heart attack, and maybe it will. But the realized benefit was surviving a rare, life-threatening event with no long-term ill effects. I remain physically active.

I went home to the care of my husband and my mother, who came to stay for a few days until I gained some mobility. I was sore from the surgery, but the pain was minimal compared to what I experienced in the throes of abdominal apoplexy. I could do very little activity, but I was able to stretch which helped me cope, physically and mentally.

I was released from medical care at the follow-up visit with the surgeon due to my rapid recovery. No more appointments or tests. He gave me one precaution related to the long incision in my abdomen "Don't do sit-ups for a few months." Best of all, he reassured me I didn't need to worry about it happening again because, "It shouldn't have happened the first time." That worked for me.

I was improving but the episode was a blow to my body which required extended time for recuperation. At first, I dreaded the several months of sick leave I faced over the summer because so much was happening at work. I had a large project scheduled to be at its busiest in June and July. Plus, I was coming up for tenure and promotion the following fall semester. I had become consumed with concern about the tenure and promotion process; not getting tenure means losing your job. I had a lot of work to do, and I wanted to get back to it. Maybe I could sneak into my office to do some work before I was fully recovered.

But I had to take it easy; recovering from major surgery is a process which should not be rushed. I decided to make the best of it. The leave proved to be a gift, providing me time to think, read, write, and reflect. People at work were inconvenienced by my absence, but the show continued without me. A tremendous burden was lifted. I discovered a full life outside of work which I had been neglecting. I did not go into work over the summer.

The months of medical time off began to feel like a holiday, and I resolved to vacation regularly in the future. My joke to friends was, "Next time I will just take time off and skip the surgery!" The upsetting work events came into perspective and lost power over me. I attended to relationships as the highest priority and focused on a healthier work/life balance. Compared to dying, not getting tenure was no big deal; the worry dissipated. I was tenured the following year. Eventual retirement became something I looked forward to.

When I returned to work in August, I asked a nurse colleague a silly question: "If I were a cat, how many of my nine lives did I use up with abdominal apoplexy?" Without hesitation she answered, "Seven." I promised myself to live those two remaining lives as fully as possible.

IV

Letting Go

First fall, then winter. Then this long pause. And then the starting over. And then the never-ending.

—"Two Ember Days in Alabama,"
Andrew Hudgins

In "Letting Go" the perspective shifts from places and events to the celebration of family members. I am fortunate that many adults—aunts, uncles, parents of friends, and close family friends—nurtured my upbringing and created many good memories that I treasure. This section features Momma and Daddy, along with their mothers, Grandmother Tulls and Grandmother Lessie, all of whom have passed on.

My parent and grandmothers were always there from early in life, more than met my needs, provided a safe and rich environment, and guided me through word and example. They were not perfect, but they were unfailing in love and caring. Even though they are gone from this world, memories endure, and I carry them as part of myself. It is a great comfort.

Memory and Loss

You will always have the memories.

That's what people said in condolence when Momma died. But if I get dementia as my mother did, memories will dissipate, and eventually I won't recognize the people who are closest to me. The ability to remember the past provides us history and context, connects us to each other, and links the past and present to the future. It defines who we are as humans and creates continuity. But what happens when a person's memory no longer works?

Human memory not affected by disease involves encoding, storing, retaining, and recalling information. Short-term or working memory stores information for less than a minute and becomes long-term when recollections are rehearsed and associated with previous, meaningful experience in a process known as consolidation. Long-term memory is enduring, but it doesn't store information like books in a library, files in a cabinet, or even lists of facts and events on a document. Instead, we retrieve pieces of memories from different places in the brain and effectively reconstruct them on the fly each time the memory is recalled, like assembling a collage. Memory is also malleable. After being recalled, the memory must be reconsolidated into storage, and thus changes each time it is recollected and returned to storage.

Momma's older memories persisted, but she had difficulty with more recent ones. She remembered family members from long ago but not that they had died, so they were part of her daily experience. She didn't hallucinate or see ghosts, she just kept asking where they were and what they were doing. It was best to say, honestly, that I hadn't seen them lately. Upon hearing they had passed away, Momma re-experienced the loss, and there was no need for that. Momma lived in the moment with no short-term memory. If I left the room after conversing with her and returned three minutes later, she greeted me as though I had been gone for weeks.

With the loss of time partitions in her brain and her short-term memory, past and present merged. When I visited, I never knew where in time she would be or who I would be. If she were living long ago, I was her younger sister. It was initially unnerving for me, but if I went with the flow without correcting her, our interactions were seamless and meaningful. After I learned to accept the time-traveling-*now*, we had rich conversations from perspectives I'd never experienced. The encounter was surreal if the topic of conversation was me—while participating in the exchange as someone else, I eavesdropped on a discussion about myself.

If our memories define us, had Momma become someone else in those final years? Was she no longer a complete person? Was she no longer my mother? I rejected these possibilities. Clearly, she had changed, but I could feel her enduring essence and her love. We don't hold developmental shortcomings against newborns. Similarly, Momma had no control over the progression of the brain damage that would ultimately take her life. She was no less a person, no less deserving of respect, and no less my mother. Her inner star was still shining. I would love whoever she was at the time, because now was all that we had.

Losing Momma to dementia caused me to rethink the meaning of personhood. We think of people as separate entities especially in western cultures, but Momma's experience showed me that human beings are not simply individuals. We are members of groups, part of a network, or constellation of people. Our linkages with each other define us, and Momma was linked to many—these connections were not severed by brain disease. Her memory had failed but no one who knew her forgot who she was or her history. We carried her with the amazing memories she had created for us, preserving her personhood in the collective Momma-who-lives-within us.

During her life Momma was a central figure in her network of family and friends—the person you seek to get things done, to find things out. She was one of the brightest stars in the constellation. When she got dementia, those closest to her took over her tasks and kept the family intact. Daddy astounded me with his ability to take on new social roles, tasks, and routines to keep it together.

When Momma died and her star collapsed, memories remained but left a vast, dark vacuum. I feared losing my early recollections of her, of the person she was, as though her loss created a black hole that would pull everything about her into oblivion. The deep pain I experienced in grief reflected the deep love that binds her to me. The relationship with Momma necessarily changed, but the internalized connection remains strong. Stars in the constellation slowly realigned, preserving collective remembrances.

Daddy remained deeply attached to Momma after she died. The bond between them transcended the barrier of death. He felt her presence, especially at night, though he knew she was gone and wasn't there physically. His pastor advised him to let her go, but he could not understand why he should.

It all came crashing down for me nearly six years later when Daddy died. His final year and particularly the last few months were difficult, but compared to Momma's ten-year decline with dementia, it seemed sudden, and I was unprepared. It has now been nearly two years since he left, and I still feel his stark absence. Losing Daddy also severed the strongest living connection with Momma.

There was an undeniable double black hole left in the network of family and friends. But the bonds among family and friends are powerful and provide stability, and the connections among the stars hold the heavens in place. There is pain, but life goes on, as it was meant to, and though it is never the same, it can be good.

Familial Flora

My mother and grandmothers loved growing plants. They spent hours cultivating yard-sized paradises during my childhood. My mother's mother had a formal approach to gardening, toiling for hours to *make* things work out. My father's mother style was practical; she believed hard work should yield food to eat and flowers to arrange in vases for others to enjoy. Momma's eclectic, informal method reflected her appreciation of beauty in the ordinary and confidence that *things will work out*. The gardens they nurtured in the past thrive in my memory, each garden revealing something about its caretaker.

*   *   *

Everyone called my mother's mother Tulls; she lived within the town limits of Walterboro. Her plentiful flower beds surrounded her house and bordered the periphery of the yard. She frequently strolled around the grounds, savoring the beauty. I accompanied her on many garden tours; she named each plant and explained its requirements. These details were of less than riveting interest for me as a child, but I loved being with Tulls. The irreplaceable time with my mother's mother was well-spent—I absorbed her desire to nurture growing things. There were too many plants and bushes to remember and name. But when I encounter foliage or flower now, I am often surprised when its name pops into my head. Perhaps I absorbed more from Tulls' botanical lectures than I realized.

I remember her persimmon tree and its exotic fruit which fascinated me. Tulls grew it for the pleasure of seeing the unusual orange-colored fruit ornamenting the tree; I don't remember anyone eating or cooking them. I was curious but never worked up the courage to taste the odd-looking persimmon. Another one of her unusual plants captivated me as well. In a shady bed in front of her house she planted elephant ears, which grew large, green, heart-shaped leaves much bigger than dinner plates. There were also similar-shaped caladiums with smaller white and red leaves etched in green. This early exposure began my lifelong fascination with intriguing foliage plants.

There were houseplants, too, especially on Tulls' back porch. One of my favorites was grown for its unique jointed stem-like green leaves cascading down the sides of the pot; Tulls called it a string plant. I have one on my front porch grown from a cutting Momma saved from Tulls' plant. My plant cascades three feet over the edge of the pot and produces tiny white blooms. Tulls died in 1995, and she had this plant for many years before, so my clone is at least four

or five-decades old. I have recently learned this succulent is called a mistletoe cactus, but it will always be a string plant to me.

Tulls was most proud of her camellias, which bloomed in cooler weather. Her bushes were loaded with reds, pinks, whites, and mixed colors. She would pick one perfect camellia and display it in a flat vase in her living room. I knew these flowers were special if Tulls would display just one at a time.

The camelia is Tulls' flower; it symbolizes perfection and excellence. This describes her approach to life—she kept her home clean and tastefully decorated and her yard groomed and exquisitely landscaped; she would even sweep the street in from of her house. She was often eyeing needed improvements in her neighbors' yards. Tulls was a loyal friend and caretaker. A perfect, exquisite camellia.

*   *   *

Grandmother Lessie, my father's mother, or "Gramp" as we called her, lived in the same rural community we did, about half a mile away. Her approach to plants was mostly utilitarian. She grew mostly vegetables: onions, cucumbers, tomatoes, beans, peas, sweet peppers, and hot peppers. Gramp spent many hours working in the garden well into her 80s. She was an old-fashioned country cook, and her produce was a mainstay in her dishes. When I was little, she prepared large weekday meals at noon for the farm-working men in the family, each daily spread equal to a lavish Sunday dinner.

Gramp preserved vegetables for the winter months, canning and freezing string beans, butter beans, and corn. She loved to make pickles and tomato and pepper relish, particularly late in summer. She put foods preserved in jars on shelves on the back porch. Outside the porch was a large fig tree growing in her back yard which produced sweet, dark figs. Gramp made preserves from the fig tree growing in her yard, as well as jellies and jams. Gramp's fig preserves on vanilla ice cream was one of Daddy's favorites. She gathered and picked out pecans from the trees in her yard. They freeze well, and we used the nuts in desserts year-round.

Gramp grew colorful zinnias and gladioli for flower arrangements and was especially proud of the glads. The tall stalks packed with blooms get top heavy and tend to fall over while growing. Gramp fretted over ways to keep them upright. Although Gramp passed away in 1994, in my mind I still see her elegant gladioli with spiked green leaves displayed in a white metal basket below the center pulpit while she beamed with satisfaction in a front pew at Doctors Creek Baptist Church.

The gladiolus, which represents strength of character, faithfulness, honor, and conviction, is Gramp's flower. She was a devout Christian and active in her church her whole life. She didn't just put on a show for Sunday—religion was her guide to daily living. To many people, she was the face of Doctors Creek Baptist Church. Gramp was a model for a well-lived life of faith. A perfect, upright gladiolus.

*   *   *

Momma's daffodils and crocuses bloomed in January, and her burgundy, yellow, and purple pansies in fall and winter. These facts are why a rhyme from a grade school writing exercise, "April showers bring May flowers," confused me; we always had flowers and a lot of rain, too. The person who wrote that line was clearly not from Lowcountry South Carolina.

Pansies and violets surrounded azalea bushes in dappled light under the live oak trees in the front yard. The azaleas added pink and lavender petals in the spring. I sometimes took pansies to my elementary school teachers, and I once picked quite a few azalea blooms as a gift for Momma. Her reaction to this well-intended denuding of her blossoms was decidedly mixed.

We had a prolific vegetable garden with tomatoes, peppers, beans, squash, okra, eggplant, and corn. These early childhood plots were mid-sized compared to Daddy's later, truck-farm sized endeavors. But they produced plenty of food which we ate fresh in season and froze for use in the winter. Momma also planted strawberries. Nothing compared to eating the sweet, sun-warmed red fruit while standing barefooted in the warm dirt of Momma's garden.

I loved the bright yellows, oranges, and reds of summer poppies, marigolds, zinnias, daylilies, roses, and verbena Momma planted in the sunny beds between the house yard and barnyard. Once I studied the daylilies for a week to confirm each blossom lasted only one day. Another favorite was baby's breath, which Momma used in arrangements. It captivated me because a close look showed each flower was a miniature bouquet of tiny white blooms; I still find small things delightful. I also liked seeing spider lilies which blossomed infrequently; they were shaped like upside-down, many-legged red spiders. I imagined they could leap from their leafless stems and scamper away; maybe this was why we didn't see them more often.

There were two dangerous but exciting plants in the yard. My sister, brother, and I were often warned to stay away from the pyracantha and the castor bean plant. The thorny pyracantha in the front had mildly poisonous orange-red berries, but I saw birds eating them. The castor bean plant was taller than me and grew near the house in the backyard. I was impressed by its large reddish, multi-lobed leaves and curious, spine-covered bean pods; the beans contain the toxin ricin which can been lethal if chewed and swallowed. Castor oil, the familiar laxative, comes from its beans.

Momma's flowering trees included the crepe myrtle with its smooth bark and deep pink-burgundy flower clusters, the mimosa with its pink powder puff blooms, and the chinaberry with its small, fragrant lavender blossoms. The first hummingbird I saw was feeding at the mimosa tree in the backyard, and the chinaberry provided the treehouse home. There was an apple tree which produced delightfully tart, blotchy-green apples. A pear tree produced large numbers of dense green pears; its fruit-laden branches nearly touched the ground.

A mulberry tree growing in the hen enclosure yielded mulberries which would fall and ferment on the ground. The chickens enjoyed this gift from above. We watched with amusement as they staggered about their pen in a drunken stupor. Blue Jays and other birds stole a few nips of fermented fruit from the chicken yard. Birds, like people, seem to enjoy a little overindulgence.

Our garden had room for camellias, gardenias, abelia, ligustrum, holly, nandina, and bay. These evergreen shrubs provided a verdant backdrop to childhood play. The regal camellias blossomed in cooler weather, but I looked forward to warmer weather when gardenias, ligustrum, and abelia flowered. The gentle fragrance of the small, pale pink abelia flowers attracted sphinx moths, which look and act like hummingbirds. The first time I saw one at Momma's abelia in early summer I stared in amazement at the intriguing insect and wondered if it were a cross between a hummingbird and a bee. I especially enjoyed the gardenia, with delicate white petals, dark green foliage, and subtle fragrance;

they always made me think of Momma. The sweet scents of early spring transport me to these magical moments in childhood.

The gardenia is Momma's flower. After she died on February 8, 2013, I planted a white garden featuring them in her honor. The gardenia signifies purity, sweetness, and joy. I cannot think of a better reflection on my mother's loving acceptance and joie de vivre. She happily cared for three children, a husband, pets, livestock, house, and yard while working as a legal secretary and then business manager. She was an exceptional human being. A perfect, fragrant gardenia.

*   *   *

My garden has a tomato, pepper, eggplant, and basil plant, each in a large pot. I have red and purple verbena, pink fringe flower, and yellow-red lantana in the back, as well as Momma's white garden. Shrubs around my house were chosen for showy and bright foliage. I also enjoy growing attractive weeds, at least for a while, reflecting my mother's laid-back style. The front yard has more mulch than grass. My house plants thrive on a successful approach to benign neglect; the snake plant is over 45 years old and one Christmas cactus is over 43. I practice garden-lite compared to Tulls' designed garden, Gramp's food cultivation, and Momma's plant profusion. But from them I adopted a practical approach to growing a variety of vegetables, colorful blooming plants, and attractive foliage. They would be proud of the miniature gardens I make as gifts or for fundraisers, each one a unique variety of small plants and succulents. My approach to gardening reflects my urban setting and lifestyle. Thanks to my female forebears, my childhood memories and love for plants are as deep and wide as my roots in the Lowcountry South Carolina soil.

Grandmother Lessie—Gramp

Iwrote the poem below in November of 1981 in celebration of my Grandmother Lessie's birthday. The sentiment of my childhood poem still holds true – I remember my Grandmother Lessie, known as Gramp to her grandchildren, as vividly now as I did at that time.

When my life is too much
And nothing goes my way
When all seems so pointless
I go to a past day.

I visit Gramp's kitchen
Lick batter from the bowl
She cooks Sunday dinner
And again I feel whole.

I can hear Gramp whistle
As she moves all about
To feed the working men
And then I feel no doubt.

I think of Gramp's chickens
I hear the distant train
Her house is so roomie
At night I might hear rain.

To Gramp on your birthday
Thanks for the yesterdays
I wish you the comfort
You gave me—for always.

My father's mother, Lessie Estelle Parker, was born November 27, 1897, in Barnwell, South Carolina, to George Washington Parker and Sallie Lula Wooley Parker. She had eight siblings including a twin brother, Jesse Washington Parker and one sibling who died as an infant. Lessie Parker married Homer Vardell Saunders in 1924. They lived in the rural community of Stokes and had four children, including Vivian Louise who died in infancy, Annie Jeanette, my father William Homer, and Betty Lou. Grandfather Homer died several weeks after I turned two in 1954. Gramp continued to live in Stokes.

Gramp told me my grandfather adored me. I was the first of six grandchildren and the only one Homer knew. I have two dream-like memories of his carrying me in his arms. In one we visited Joe Butler's country food store and hangout. I remember looking around the store from Granddaddy's arms while he and Joe talked. In the other recollection Granddaddy and I were on the porch of a rural neighbor, the Stokarskis, while he and Mr. Stokarski talked. The feeling that remains from these treasured memories is being carried by his love.

I remember taking naps in the afternoons in Lessie's country home constructed of wood with its large rooms and high ceilings. Gramp's house was farther from the railroad track than ours, which made the train whistle seem distant and sad as I drifted to sleep. I rested well, covered by a quilt handmade by her mother and sisters. My sister, brother, and I still enjoy this original quilt, which was restored and divided into three smaller quilts by an accomplished seamstress friend. When I use it now, I imagine my younger self sleeping soundly under it more than 50 years ago, a comforting connection with the past.

Grandmother Lessie was a fixture at the family church, Doctors Creek Baptist. A 1982 article in the Walterboro weekly newspaper, *The Press and Standard*, reported that she had taught a Sunday school class for 50 years. She took a leadership role in women's missions and was a persuasive advocate for donations to church mission offerings. A devout Christian woman, she believed attendance at church was the cornerstone of a life well-lived. Gramp expected everyone to be at the church when its doors opened on Sunday mornings and evenings, and Wednesday evenings. Ms. Lessie, as she was known at church, also expected Doctors Creek Baptist to adhere to its end of the bargain by strictly following its schedule. Lessie did not approve of sermons running later than 12 noon on Sunday and declared, "The Lord can do His work between 11 am and 12 noon."

Lessie had little tolerance for strong language or the use of alcohol. In the mid-1960s she opposed the innovation of distributing soft drinks in cans rather than bottles because it was too much like cans of beer. She was ahead of her time in calling cigarettes, "Coffin nails." My grandmother did not put on strong displays of emotion, but she did state her point of view.

Gramp wrote the Doctors Creek Community weekly column to *The Press and Standard* for nearly 30 years, beginning in 1962. This was one of many community columns which kept subscribers informed of local church, community, and family events and celebrations, as well as losses. She actively sought news from Doctors Creek members and Stokes residents, and we all had to be careful when she was in this mode. Daddy once commented that he was afraid to go to the bathroom for fear that, "It will end up in *The Press and Standard*." I was proud of Lessie's column. She was a faithful and consistent contributor and never missed a column or a meeting.

An exceptional southern cook, Grandmother Lessie spent a lot of time in the kitchen, whistling while she worked. She often fixed dinner on Sundays, but I remember most the large midday meal she cooked for the working men, including Daddy, Uncle Bub, Uncle John, and other relatives. One of her homemade specialties was chicken or ham pie. It was made in lasagna-sized casserole dishes and was like chicken and dumplings except Lessie used made-from-scratch biscuits instead of dumplings.

My meal preparation task around age 10 was to get ice for the glasses, which would then be filled with sweetened iced tea. Long before the days of automatic icemakers, this was a difficult job, because I had to firmly pull up on a handle to release the ice from each of several metal trays. The handle was frozen to the tray and the ice stuck in the tray. It hurt my hands to work with it. It was a little easier job when Gramp showed me how to run water over the entire contraption to get the handle and ice free. The sweetened iced tea made it all worth it.

Gramp often baked cakes and we youngsters looked forward to licking the brown ceramic batter bowl. Grandmother Lessie scraped the bowl nearly clean before handing it over to her eager grandchildren. I wished she would've let more batter remain in the bowl rather than putting it all in the cake. After all, the batter was better than the finished cake! But her baked goods, especially coconut cake, didn't last long either. Lessie fretted over icing being too runny, but I didn't see the problem. It tasted good—who cared if it didn't look good? When I started baking, I understood why Lessie cared about how the final product looked as well as tasted. But I am less careful about scraping batter from the bowl if bowl-licking youngsters are nearby waiting for a treat.

When I was little, it worried me that Grandmother Lessie lived by herself. I knew my Grandfather died years earlier, and she had no one else living with her in what seemed to be a large, empty place. I had many conversations with her about this. Her response to my concern was, "I am alone but never lonely." This appeased me briefly, and I often thought about what she said. I didn't fully understand the meaning until later in life when I learned to experience closeness with loved ones without their physical presence.

Gramp raised chickens for eggs to sell. I looked forward to the spring when she would get a new batch of biddies. They were kept in a special, warm brooder house with a large heated metal hood hanging from the ceiling under which the chicks gathered for warmth. It was a substitute for the protective momma hen collecting the babies under her wings. I loved walking into the brooder room, standing among what seemed like hundreds of chicks and hearing the cacophony of their peeps. I had to be careful moving around, though, because the tiny birds got underfoot. In no time, the peeps grew into pullets and then full-grown hens.

Grandmother Lessie was protective of her hens, which are not known for their smarts. They don't always seek shelter in rainstorms, and Gramp often intervened, because she believed they would look up into the sky and drown. I have a vivid memory of one of these storms. Bolts of lightning flashed frequently overhead with instantaneous claps of thunder. Visibility was limited to a few feet by the heavy, driving rain. I stood on Lessie's screened back porch while Lessie risked her life herding hens in the chicken yard, and the remainder of the family was stuck in a car parked in the driveway. I was completely immobilized in fear, terrified lightning would strike Gramp or me. I could not go inside the house leaving Gramp outside and was unable to brave the short distance from the porch to the safety of the car.

On another occasion, I was safely seated in Lessie's house during a storm when a nearby explosion and crack of thunder shook the house and my being. I'd never heard or felt anything like it. Quite frightened, I jumped up and ran to the window. Lightning had struck the nearby Sycamore tree in her yard, instantly vaporized the moisture inside the tree and obliterated it. It is no wonder I had a fear of lightning storms when I was small.

Lessie enjoyed excellent health most of her life, but her body began letting her down as she aged. Her hearing was poor for many years, and sometimes we could not get her attention if she were alone in the house. Then her vision began failing, and she became less nimble. She was unable to see clearly or turn her head to view the surroundings. This resulted in her pulling in front of oncoming cars. It was a stressful time when Daddy took away her car keys.

She had trouble getting in and out of her old-fashioned bathtub with legs. Aunt Betty, her daughter, contacted social services to evaluate her eligibility to receive services. Gramp had a remarkable ability to rally briefly when the circumstances required it. The agility of her youth returned for the duration of the assessment—placing a hand on the side of the tub, she hopped in and out—making her ineligible for the needed services and leaving Aunt Betty displeased.

Daddy and Aunt Betty became concerned about their mother staying at home alone. So, for a brief time Lessie lived with Momma and Daddy as well as with Aunt Betty. But she became increasingly frail and eventually required professional care in the local nursing home. Her memory became less sharp, due in large part to institutional living, but her mind and sense of humor remained intact. During a visit, my father asked her what she had for lunch. She paused thoughtfully and said, "I can't remember, but I hope it was fried chicken."

Lessie was proud of getting old and wanted to live until she reached 100. But time caught up with Gramp, robbing her of the independence she had enjoyed for so many years and leaving her confined to a bed. Toward the end she said to Daddy, "I don't know why the Lord hasn't called me home." Lessie Parker Saunders received her call June 5, 1994, at the age of 96, after a long life well-lived. Memories of her still comfort me.

Grandmother Tulls

Momma named me Ruth Prentiss Saunders in honor of her mother whose maiden name was Ruth Prentiss. This reflected the deep connection between my mother, also named Ruth, and her mother. I feel a deep bond with both. Tulls was Ruth Prentiss Tilley when Momma and Daddy were dating. My father addressed his future mother-in-law as "Tills," and when I was small, the closest I could come was "Tulls." The name stuck and is what all members of the family called her. It was an unconventional moniker for a grandmother, but she preferred it over being called "Grandma."

Tulls was one of the more colorful members of the family. She was the only adult family member who said "damn" in front of children. This language was not common in the late 1950s and early 1960s, so I was shocked and impressed at the same time. This was a contrast to Grandmother Lessie, my father's mother, a traditionally devout woman who took a dim view of the use of strong language. At the time I thought Lessie was religious and Tulls was not. It was years before I understood there was more than one spiritual path—both grandmothers were strong women of faith.

Tulls often told a story about me when I was small. I lay in my crib under covers, with brow furrowed, arms and legs moving about. Tulls asked, "Ruthie, what are you doing?" My reply was, "I'm wrurrrying." I did not articulate the sources of my anxiety. She found it astonishing that someone as young as I was not only worrying but was able to name it. At the time she failed to make the obvious connection, that I was emulating a highly practiced, fretting adult role model: her.

Tulls worked in the Clerk of Court's Office in the Court House in Colleton County until she retired. Momma frequently took my sister, brother, and me there for brief visits during working hours. The building was impressive with large, stately rooms including the court room, and the polished granite floors lent an air of formality. I loved going to see her there and enjoyed looking through the large ledger books where handwritten records were entered.

The Clerk of Court in Colleton County supports the Circuit Court which includes Criminal and Civil cases and the Family Court. Duties include court docket management, receipt of fees and fines, maintenance of all court records, jury management, courtroom staffing, and submission of reports to state and federal agencies. In childhood I had no idea about the magnitude of responsibility that my grandmother helped manage in her work. I now appreciate how I grew up surrounded by strong, working women—positive models that served me well throughout my career.

I loved to spend the night with Tulls, who lived in the town of Walterboro. She kept her house and yard spotless which, in retrospect, made her willingness to keep her grandchildren remarkable. We were whirling dervishes leaving paths of benign destruction in our wake, but she did not complain. She did wisely keep us one at a time. My sister, brother, and I remember her living room in detail because we spent so much time there.

Her neighborhood was less than 10 miles "as the crow flies" from our rural home outside of Walterboro, but the town birds made different sounds. I enjoyed listening to them in the morning when I awoke at her house. One of them sounded like a squeaky gate opening, which I later learned was a Grackle. I looked forward to the feast she prepared for me at breakfast: all the pancakes I could eat with syrup and hot tea with milk served on fine china. I felt like royalty when I stayed with her.

Another treat at Tulls' house was the special vanilla ice cream she kept in the freezer or "ice box" as she called it. I asked for it when I would visit. It was soft and creamy, quite unlike the firmer stuff we ate. I often wondered why Momma didn't buy this variety. I know now Tulls' ice cream was exceptional because she kept the freezer temperature too high, probably an attempt to save money. But never mind that, Tulls' icebox frozen treats were in a class of their own. To this day I prefer soft, creamy ice cream.

Our family often ate Sunday dinner at Tulls' house. An excellent cook, she prepared large volumes of many dishes and was quite the hostess. She expected people to eat everything and had the habit of plopping another serving on your plate as she was asking if you wanted more. This annoyed my father, because he became caught between not wanting to eat too much and feeling compelled to clean his plate. Cleaning the plate always won.

Grandmother Tulls was generous with candy, too. At Halloween we went into town dressed in our finest costumes made from sheets and old clothes for the annual "Trick or Treat" ritual. This was always fun, and we enjoyed the bounty for days afterward. We began in Tulls' neighborhood on Warren Street. My favorite stop was Tulls' house because she always had a giant bowl with a variety of candies, and she would invite us to grab a handful. It was a thrill seeing all the candy and being able to choose exactly what I liked while taking as much as I wanted. Most adults simply threw a few pieces of candy into the trick-or-treater's bags, but Grandmother Tulls made sure everyone was fully "treated."

When Momma drove us to school in the later childhood years, we often encountered Tulls driving in the opposite direction on her way to work. She didn't just drive to work, she was bearing down with a death grip on the steering wheel, eyes riveted on the road in front of her and completely oblivious to the surrounding environment—this included a car full of close relatives waving, shouting and blowing the horn at her.

It was great entertainment for us trying to get her attention each morning. At least it was before I realized later in life that my driving style and, indeed my approach to life, are similar. This is part of the origin of my saying, "Anything worth doing is worth overdoing." I suppose people laugh at me when I am driving and that's OK. I am happy to provide a little amusement for others in the same manner as Tulls.

A corollary to the "overdoing" aphorism I learned from Tulls' example is, "If a little is good, then more is better." At first blush this may seem reasonable, but some things are beneficial in small amounts and harmful beyond that. It seemed that Tulls never quite got this as she repeatedly applied generous amounts of fertilizer to her garden. Or maybe her challenge was calibrating the proper amount. Just the same, her garden was amazing, populated by vigorously growing plants that could take a little fertilizer burn now and then.

Tulls had many friends and was a marvelous caretaker. She also had "foot in mouth" disease. When she had a thought in her head, it immediately exited her mouth. One time she and my mother encountered an old friend as they entered a restaurant. Tulls' opening greeting was, "Why, Gertrude, you're as fat as a pig!"

In her heart this was a simple statement of fact and a warm salutation. She often was surprised when people reacted negatively to her well-intended pronouncements. She later commented to my mother with characteristic naivete, "You know, Gertrude seemed a bit stiff today."

Grandmother Tulls was born in 1908 and had a difficult life early on. She was three when her mother died leaving six children. Her father remarried, but in childhood Tulls helped care for eight siblings. She took care of them in times of need later in life as well and carried this sense of responsibility until the day she left us. At age 16, Ruth Prentiss married Harold Jaillette and had three children including Harry, my mother, Ruth, and Anne. They divorced and she later married Clyde Robert Tilley but that did not work out either. Divorce was uncommon in the 1930s and not as socially acceptable as today. Yet she found work and raised her family in a loving environment surrounded by a large and close extended family.

Tulls' life bridged two cultures. When I was small, we sometimes visited her father at her childhood home by the Toogoodoo River on Yonges Island. My sister, brother, and I called him "Great Grandpa on the River." He spoke Gullah, and meaningful conversations required a translator. In one such interaction when I was nearly 13, Great Grandpa asked me if I were getting married soon. I was speechless—this was not remotely on the horizon for me. Fortunately, Tulls intervened, explained I was too young, and smoothed things over. I felt as though I had made a narrow escape.

Much later I understood I had experienced colliding cultures—Great Grandpa's world was far removed from mine. Yonges Island was a barrier island of South Carolina and in the earlier years the family lived largely in isolation, a separate world from the mainland. It was also a culture in which ghosts were a fact of life. Tulls knew her father was dying when he saw an angel by his bed. The world my Great Grandpa knew and in which my Grandmother Tulls grew up has long ceased to exist.

Tulls' innocent forthrightness and off-kilter perspective amused me when I was growing up. She was fun to be with, and I lovingly thought she lived just this side of reality. In her later, years she crossed to the other side, but due to her cultural background it was difficult to tell the precise time. My mother drew the line when her mother had a car crash, which could have been much worse if another vehicle had been involved.

Tulls was uninjured and when asked to describe what happened explained, "An angel was driving the car." In mainstream society this sounded like dementia, but from the perspective of her upbringing this was a valid explanation of how she started in one parking lot, shot across a city street, and collided with a building without injury. She eventually moved to a nursing home to receive care. She did not know where she was and expressed surprise that anyone could find her. She talked about wanting to go home, and I wished that she could return to her long-time Walterboro residence. I eventually realized the home she desired was inhabited by her deceased loved ones and existed only in her past.

I treasure the memory of the last visit my husband and I had with her. She knew me but was not sure about my husband. In her mind he might have been my father, and perhaps I was a younger version of myself. She welcomed us into her room with the warmth of a gracious southern hostess. She explained how she was lucky to have found such a nice place where she could eat and where she had a bed. I don't remember other details of the conversation, but Tulls was happy and light, enjoying our company with laughter as from earlier days.

My Grandmother Tulls passed away on February 6, 1995, at the age of 86. She was buried in the St. Paul's Episcopal Cemetery on Yonges Island, SC, where she grew up. As her casket was lowered into the ground on that cold, winter day, I sensed she had finally made it home.

Momma

My mother's full name was Ruth Otis Jaillette Saunders, though she most often went by Ruth Saunders. Her husband, granddaughters, and friends called her Ruth. Daddy stretched her name into two syllables when he called her from the back of the house, "Ru---uth!" Her children called her Momma, younger generations knew her as Ms. Ruth, and other family members addressed her as Sis, Tutta, or Aunt Tutta. "Tutta" was her younger sister's attempt at saying "sister," and the name stuck. A person with many roles earns many names.

Born on December 16, 1926 to Ruth Prentiss Jaillette and Harold West Jaillette, Ruth Otis Jaillette grew up near the Toogoodoo River, a tidal river on Yonge's Island in Charleston County, South Carolina. She moved with her mother, older brother and younger sister to Walterboro in 1936 after her parents divorced. She married William H. Saunders in 1949 and they moved to the rural community of Stokes in 1951. I was born a year later, followed by my sister Russell Anne two years later, and brother Billy four years after that.

I benefited from Momma's sage advice from early on. At preschool age I played with wooden puzzles with animal shapes that fit into the appropriate animal slots. One time I took a notion the giraffe piece should go into the elephant slot. This did not work, but I was a determined and goal-oriented tot and hammered on it, becoming more upset as the giraffe refused to morph. Momma intervened, "Ruthie, take your time to look at the pieces and find the shape that fits. Then it is easy to put in place." Another time I became frustrated while drawing a picture and repeatedly balled up and threw partial sketches away. Momma explained, "A *real* artist finishes the work before deciding what to do with it." This was probably an effort to save paper but helped me learn to cope with my impatience.

Momma's dedication to family and home showed in her daily actions. She planted and cultivated flower and vegetable gardens, minded pets and chickens, painted walls, varnished floors, and laid brick around the house foundation in addition to cleaning, sweeping floors, washing clothes, and cooking meals. I remember her carrying me from the house to the car and then into the doctor's office more than once when I was too sick to walk. If it needed to be done, she did it.

Ordinary things were fun with Momma, like the "butterfly" sandwiches she made when I was small. She trimmed the crust, cut the bread in half diagonally and put the triangles point-to-point in the shape of a butterfly. She found creative solutions to mundane problems. I ran out of glue for a project and Momma showed me how to improvise using flour and water. When her skirt hem came loose at work, she stapled it as a temporary measure. If she spilled food on her blouse and couldn't change right away, she put it on backwards and wore her jacket or sweater over it.

Silverware and fine china were not "good" things to save for use on special occasions in our household. Everything was available for routine use—Momma believed in living every day. She allowed us to dig in the yard with silver serving spoons. We inadvertently left some of them buried, like treasures to be discovered in later years. Unlike her mother, Momma thought scrubbing pots until they were shiny was a waste of time and energy—they just needed to be clean. Over time Momma's pots and baking pans took on a bronzy, baked-in sheen, which added to their charm.

The wild creatures that inhabited the Lowcountry captivated Momma, especially birds. She and Daddy kept bird feeders filled year-round and hummingbird feeders up during the warm months. At the peak of summer, they had a hundred or more hummers. They observed waterfowl from a shelter on their small woodland pond. Momma became skilled at identifying birds living year-round in the Lowcountry as well as migratory species.

Stray animals found a home with Momma, and she adopted many dogs and cats over the years. She didn't give them creative names: Stray was a yellow dog that wandered up, Stripe was a black dog adorned with a white stripe around the neck, and Mailbox was a generic black and brown dog that someone dropped off at the, you guessed it, mailbox. One stray, named by my best friend, was called Samantha, because the dog twitched her nose like the TV witch of the same name. Even our "good" dogs and cats were misfits and castaways, such as Sport the hunting dog who was afraid of gunfire.

All human beings were friends – skin color, station in life, and income level made no difference to Momma. She looked into people's eyes and saw their hearts. A childhood experience in the 1930s shaped the way she felt about race. She saw an African American mother and child walking on the sidewalk in the small town of Walterboro. The child tripped, skinned her knee, and cried to her mother as her knee bled. Momma saw the blood, felt the girl's pain, and realized there was no difference between her and this child. This may seem obvious today, but in the 1930s segregated South it was quite a realization for a white child. Together, Momma and Daddy raised us with the view that all people are equal and deserve respect.

With a diploma from the Florence Business College, Momma worked as a legal secretary and court recorder in Walterboro for many years before she and Daddy managed the booming family business, Saunders Farm Supply. Because of her business acumen, there was no form Ruth Saunders could not complete. She helped community members with taxes, legal documents and other paperwork and provided Notary Public services.

Momma's fascination with local history led her to research and preserve ways of life that no longer existed. She examined old documents, conducted interviews, and compiled histories of our family church, Doctors Creek Baptist, founded in 1837, and the local Stokes and Rhodes Still communities. An adept storyteller, she enrolled in college English classes in her 60s at the Walterboro Salkehatchie branch of the University of South Carolina with the goal of writing stories for future generations. Being the only older adult in a classroom of college students was daunting to her. She performed adequately on the written tests, but with years of storytelling and life experience Momma excelled on writing assignments. Some of her work was published in local newspapers, and she self-published many of her pieces in a book for others to enjoy, *Low Country Children*.

When my brother was in high school, Momma ran for and was elected to the Colleton County School Board as its second female member. This was shortly after the Supreme Court mandated school consolidation in South

Carolina, which was intended to accomplish what earlier desegregation efforts had failed to achieve. It was a challenging time to work in education. She served for 20 years, including eight years as Chair.

During the final years of her life, the person I knew as Momma evolved due to the progression of dementia. This is a fate her mother and other women in her family suffered and was something she feared and dreaded. The transition period when she was aware of her decline was difficult, and both Momma and Daddy hid it—as much from themselves as from us—until she forgot basic things such as how to type and cook.

In the early phases of dementia, Momma lived at home, and Daddy gradually took over all household duties as well as taking care of her. These were stressful times. I visited from my home in Columbia on weekends. She was confused, wandered about, and didn't want to take baths. She packed odd items into numerous accumulated pocketbooks and sorted through bags, drawers, and closets.

Daddy was not equipped to handle someone with dementia—it was not good for her and took a toll on him—but he wanted to keep her at home. Finally, my sister, brother, and I persuaded him to place her in institutional care. By the time Momma left she did not recognize her decades-long place of residence as home. She went to The Oaks, a Methodist home in Orangeburg, about a 40-minute drive from Stokes.

After an initial adjustment period at the nursing home, Momma's quality of life improved. Daddy visited three or four times per week and family members filled in the other days for the entire time she was there. She delighted in seeing the nesting birds in the oversized cage in the lobby and visiting the cats residing at The Oaks. Family members took her outdoors to sit by the on-site pond and to see the flower gardens. When not with family, she talked with the staff at the nursing station who enjoyed interacting with her.

There was a fitness class for the residents at The Oaks on my regular visit day. I volunteered as an exercise leader, the Fitness Fairy. This entailed dressing up in pink tights and a tutu, donning wings, and carrying a wishing-you-wellness wand while leading the class. It was fun being with Momma and the other residents. I have missed being the Fitness Fairy and especially seeing the smiles from the ladies and men in the group. Sometimes they stopped me in the dining room to ask, "Aren't you the exercise butterfly?"

Even as her dementia progressed, Momma saw the positive and beauty in everything. One day as I pushed her through the nursing home in her wheelchair, she fixed her gaze on the janitor's cart with the comment, "Isn't that lovely!" She became a younger version of herself with her natural sweetness intensified. Dementia can change personality in negative ways, but her essential nature did not change.

I marveled at Momma's social graces while at The Oaks. She didn't know where she was or who the people were, but that was not important—she smiled and was polite and appreciative of others. She gave everyone a royal wave as I rolled her wheelchair through the halls. Many didn't realize she had advanced dementia. Her final lesson was important: all we have is now and now matters most for love.

On a visit near the end, she said to me "It is hard, so hard, so hard, so very hard." I understood and said, "Momma, you have done your part. You can go when you are ready." Shortly afterward she refused to eat. Her Living Will was clear—no tubes to prolong her life. We placed her on hospice. Three days later, February 8, 2013, Momma was gone. I have grieved the loss of at least two people: the mother I had known and loved all my life and the person I came to know and love in the final three years.

The funeral and burial were a blur to me. When most people had left the burial tent, I gave her casket three little pats. A hug and a pat-pat-pat on the back was a signal of her love. My brother put a birdfeeder at her gravesite to honor her love of birds. Shortly after the funeral, I visited her grave and saw a painted bunting, one of Momma's favorites, at the bird feeder. The painted bunting is a striking bird, tinted blue, green, yellow and red, as if by the hand of God. I felt Momma comforting me, even in death. In her own words:

I hope when I die that my friends and relatives will gather and mourn a little bit, and then go on to remember the many good, funny and special things that we shared and enjoyed.

— From the story "Uncle John"
in Low Country Children, 1986, by Ruth [J.] Saunders

Daddy

Bull, Mr. Billy, Daddy, and Poppa Bear were all names for my father, William Homer Saunders. The nickname Bull was given to him when he played football in high school and came from his tendency to put his head down and push ahead no matter what obstacles were blocking the way. This sometimes came across as stubbornness, which could be frustrating, but his Bull nature served him well throughout life. He was known as "Mr. Billy" to most people in the community, reflecting a Southern blend of formality and informality. The title "Mr." showed respect and recognized his social position as a farm business owner and community leader, and the nickname "Billy" was what his family and close friends called him. The name "Daddy" or "Dad" was used exclusively by his three children, although in the final years one of his dear caretakers also called him "Daddy." His children sometimes referred to him as "Poppa Bear," typically in his absence. It reflected his teddy bear side, as well as his occasional tendency to growl when in certain moods.

Daddy was born in the rural community of Stokes, South Carolina on March 23rd, 1928, in the home of his parents, Homer Vardell Saunders and Lessie Parker Saunders, and spent nearly his entire life within one mile of his birthplace. Not many people today are so thoroughly a lifelong member of a geographic community. He was away from Stokes only three times: a brief time serving in the Pacific Theater of Operations in the U.S. Marine Corps., near the end of World War II when he enlisted slightly underage; a briefer time at the Citadel in Charleston, SC after military service and high school; and a short time in apartments in Walterboro after he and Momma married in 1949, before they bought a house in Stokes. Some years later, in the 1970s, he and Momma built a new house next door, in a rural sense, to the old house. This was his home for many years until June 22, 2018, when he entered the Veterans Victory House Nursing Home in Walterboro.

Daddy applied his Bull nature to everything that he did, especially work. In the very early days he logged timber, difficult and dangerous work. Early on, he also farmed and worked in the fertilizer business with Mr. Horace Kinsey of the Colleton Fertilizer Company. Daddy eventually started his own fertilizer business and became a commissioned agent for Royster Fertilizer Company, as well as continuing to farm.

Daddy and Momma owned and operated Saunders Farm Supply for nearly 50 years, a business they started from home. My father did a good job and was honest, fair, and dependable. I owe my work ethic and general approach to life in large part to my father. Being in the farm and fertilizer businesses meant that he had a busy season. In the spring and summer, he grew crops such as soybeans and corn and spread fertilizer for other farmers who grew other crops, including cotton and hay. During winters he grew winter wheat, so there was work going on year-round. But the spring and summer months of the busy season were off-the-scale in terms of hours of work per day. While growing up, we had many late suppers due to Daddy's long hours and our family practice of eating together. He was not afraid of hard work.

Daddy always found time for us. He would make up stories to tell us; many of them were about Felix the Cat—a cartoon character from the silent film era. Daddy probably started by recalling some actual stories from the series, but we loved Felix the Cat and demanded more and more stories, so Daddy had to improvise a lot. We took yearly family summer vacations after the busy season to spend a week at Edisto Beach, and took vacations to the mountains of North Carolina when we were older. I looked forward to these fun times with Daddy and thought this was just what fathers did. Years later, and with the sad knowledge that not all parents are as benevolent as mine were, I appreciate the creativity, energy, and time Daddy devoted to playing with us. Daddy spent time with us, went to a lot of trouble to amuse us, and enjoyed doing it. This was love in action.

Daddy was a bit of a teaser, especially when we were small. When we first went to the mountains and saw cows standing on the edge of a steep hill, Daddy explained that mountain cows had two legs shorter and two legs longer to accommodate the hills. I'm not sure we really fell for that, but it was typical of his stories. When I was growing up, I found his constant teasing to be frustrating, because it often was difficult to tell when he was serious. I was stunned, years later, to learn that I had absorbed this trait when students I was teaching commented that they could not tell when I was being serious! To be on the safe side, it seems, they took notes on anything and everything I said in class, including my "jokes."

In his later years, Daddy gained another name. His grandchildren and great-grandchildren called him Gran Gran (or something approximating that for the younger great-grandsons). He spent a lot of time with his five granddaughters and, later, with his three great-grandsons. His granddaughters helped soften his Bull side and, according to them, he was the "greatest grandfather ever." I now realize that he never forgot how to play, which is unusual in someone so focused on work.

It may not be possible for farmers to fully retire, because after retirement Daddy cultivated a several acre summer garden that included butter beans, bell peppers, squash, zucchini, okra, tomatoes, corn—a lot of sweet corn—and probably other things that I am forgetting. He also cultivated a smaller, cool-season garden that included broccoli, cauliflower, onions, cabbage, and potatoes. He produced enough vegetables to feed the community and beyond. I've eaten my share and hauled many vegetables from the Lowcountry to share with friends and family in the Midlands over the years. He tended the garden diligently, hoeing, pulling weeds, watering, and harvesting.

People looked forward to the produce, especially the corn, and Daddy gave it all away. He was known in the community for his generosity. Later in life when he became more physically challenged, he enlisted family members to continue this legacy of devotion to the garden with admittedly mixed success. Those in the immediate family, especially my brother and sister who lived near him, had to contend with Daddy's obsession that nothing goes to waste.

When you plant too much, especially stuff that proliferates such as squash, managing the excess county becomes challenging. People can eat only so much squash. And one had to be careful about just tossing it in the woods, so as not to be caught. Daddy didn't eat much from his garden—he just expected everyone else to enjoy it—every bit of it.

He was able to work in the garden until his body had almost completely let him down, because he discovered that he could do many tasks while sitting on his riding lawnmower. When his walking became unsteady, he became a whole man again when he mounted the lawnmower. He was, in-essence, part man and part machine, a sort of retired bionic farmer.

I often caught glimpses of him zooming through the yard on his lawn-mower on footage from the front door security camera at his home. At first, I was concerned because this was not a safe activity for an increasingly frail 90-year-old. Then I realized that aging had not changed his Bull nature. There was no way to stop the charging "Bull"—it was best to simply clear the path for him. He could not only cut grass but blow leaves into piles to burn. His ability to corral leaves spread across a large yard into a small, neat pile would have put a talented border collie to shame, although admittedly leaves are even less sentient than the traditional quarry of border collies. The man-and-his-machine was a master.

In the last five years of his life, which also happened to be the years he was without Momma, he contended with one health challenge after another. He suffered increased hearing loss, blockages in two coronary arteries requiring cardiac catheterization, a badly broken leg due to a fall, macular degeneration in one eye resulting in loss of vision, atrial fibrillation that required a pace-maker, increasingly severe arthritis in his foot, ankle, knee, and shoulder, a bout of pneumonia that nearly killed him, chronic obstructive pulmonary disease, congestive heart failure, chronic urinary tract infections, and severe infections in the skin on his legs. These things slowed him down, but he never stopped moving until the end. Keeping up with him wore me out when I visited from my home in Columbia. His Bull nature kept him going, perhaps at times when it would have been better for him to rest.

One of the most remarkable things about him in his later years was how he coped with the loss of his wife of over 60 years, Ruth J. Saunders. She died

February 8th, 2013, after nearly 10 years of advancing dementia. He visited her in the nursing home in Orangeburg three or four times a week for the several years she was in care, even though it was an out-of-town trip for him. My mother and my father had a very deep connection that persisted even after she was gone from this earth. He always spoke of her in the present tense, and contributions to his church were made in both names.

The decline and loss of Mom was difficult for him, but he adjusted. For most of their life together, in addition to working, my mother had done all the cooking, cleaning, and shopping, even selecting his clothes for him to wear each day. Somehow, as she became less able to manage at home and then left for the nursing home, Daddy took over the cooking, cleaning, clothes washing, and even social obligations such as sending birthday cards. This surprised me because, based on the strict labor division earlier in his marriage, I thought he would be lost without Momma. He asked one of his adult granddaughters to teach him how to clean, and he prided himself on having a clean house. It was inspiring to see him staying engaged physically, mentally, and socially. He simply did what had to be done. Having tasks to accomplish helped him cope, and it seems that he could cope with just about anything.

Daddy died on July 26, 2018, at the age of 90 and was buried in the Saunders' cemetery plot at Drs. Creek Baptist Church on August 1. The burial service at the graveside was quite remarkable. As we left the church building to walk the short distance to the adjacent cemetery, a gentle thunder signaled impending rain. As a farmer, Daddy loved rain, and I thought what a nice tribute he was getting from Mother Nature, perhaps acknowledging his love for the moist soil that nourished plants.

As we gathered under the burial tent for the U.S. Marine Corp bugle and flag ceremony at the graveside, it started raining lightly. The bugler played Taps. Then, in complete silence except for the gentle rain and thunder, two Marines slowly folded the flag that was on Daddy's casket and saluted him. Outside the tent, the air was filled with hundreds and hundreds of dragonflies flying silently around the cemetery yard. There was a sense of release and serenity, the perfect farewell for Daddy. The rain and thunder stopped shortly after the burial.

In some Native American legends, the dragonfly is a symbol of resurrection and renewal after hardship. Daddy's very last days were not easy. But, thanks to the dragonflies, I am comforted that Daddy achieved peace on that day, in August, when he came to his final rest beside Momma.

Letting Go

For me summer begins when the hummingbirds arrive and ends when they leave. I remember seeing my first hummingbird feeding at a Mimosa tree blossom in the backyard when I was a child. I marveled then, as I do now, at what wondrous creatures they are, light refracting in their feathers creating jeweled colors. They are small for birds, but quite feisty and not afraid of people, though that doesn't mean that they like us around. I wouldn't be afraid, either, if I could fly that quickly in any direction with such maneuverability. They are social birds, nearly always in the presence of other hummers, but they are also territorial and aggressive, so they don't get along with each other particularly well. Hummers, with their energy, quickness, and fierceness bundled together in such a small and beautiful package, represent *life* to me.

I associate hummingbirds with Daddy. In the mid-1970s, Momma and Daddy first put up sugar-water hummingbird feeders at their newly built, larger home next door to the home we grew up in. They initially put up two but quickly had to expand to accommodate the swelling numbers of voracious little birds. For many years they kept four to six feeders up and, in peak summer season, would have to refill them all daily. Momma and Daddy kept nectar mixtures in the refrigerator and were always prepared to refill when needed. They could see most of the feeders through the large breakfast room windows and watched them throughout the day.

If you see a hummer in South Carolina, it is more than likely a Ruby-Throated Hummingbird, since that is the main species that breeds east of the Mississippi River. They are migratory and grace us with their lively presence during the warm months of the year. Momma and Daddy's first couple arrived on or near Daddy's birthday, March 23. We called these birds "scouts" because they arrived ahead of the multiple dozens that would feed later in the summer. The hummers leave abruptly by the first week in October on their long migratory journey to Southern Mexico and Central America. Momma and Daddy enjoyed feeding and watching hummingbirds together for many summers.

Daddy kept up the hummingbird-feeding tradition after Momma moved to the nursing home in 2010 and after she passed away in 2013. He did this as a memorial to Momma and her love of all birds, but Daddy also loved them. He spent hours observing them and recognized individual birds based on their patterns of behavior, as well as nuanced differences in their coloration. He was diligent in feeding the hummers and kept a running tally of how many pounds of sugar he purchased for them.

As his health declined, Daddy enlisted the help of family members to keep the hummingbirds fed. He *expected* us to help with the hummingbirds, so it was more like an unspoken demand than a direct request, although he was not shy about giving orders to get things done.

I visited Daddy as much as I could in the final months before he entered the nursing facility at age 90. Naturally, I helped care for the hummingbirds (as did other family members) and continued to do so after he left home, even though I live in Columbia, about 90 miles away from his Stokes home outside of Walterboro. I kept up the routine for a while after he passed away in July 2018, which was not difficult, as I made frequent trips to visit family.

During August, I became increasingly aware that it was time to let Daddy's little birds go. There were plenty of nectar-filled flowers and other feeders in the rural community to sustain them. But I hesitated to relinquish this task, because Daddy had much in common with his hummers. They were both assertive, feisty, focused on getting the task at hand done, and remarkably consistent in their behavior. These connections made it difficult, but I was able to let the hummingbirds go by September.

I visited Daddy's house several months later and noticed that the feeders were still hanging even though the hummingbirds had migrated for the fall—the empty feeders reminded me that the birds were gone. Suddenly, I was overwhelmed with a wave of intense grief, reexperiencing in full the absolute absence of my father, knowing he would not return.

It is sad saying a temporary goodbye to the hummers; it is much more difficult to let go of Daddy. Yet, there is some comfort knowing the energetic and task-obsessed birds he loved will come back every year.

V

Triple Star System

Our most treasured family heirloom are our sweet family memories.
The past is never dead, it is not even past.

—William Faulkner

Triple Star System

Scientists believe many of the stars in the universe occur in threes. These stars are gravitationally bound to each other and orbit the point of equilibrium of their gravitational fields. Often, two orbit each other in a binary system and the third orbits the pair at a larger distance. This forms a stable arrangement that may last billions of years. Alpha Centauri, the closest star and planetary systems at 4.37 light years from the sun, is a triplet. Difficult to see from earth, these structures may appear to a single luminous body. But scientists know the stars are there because of the effects they have on each other. As one goes behind the other, light intensity dips. Uneven timing in these dips indicates the presence of at least three heavenly bodies. In other cases, the gravitational pull of an unseen orb may cause an observable wobble in its companion. Even if they cannot be directly observed, companion stars influence each other.

I remember when at age two my single star existence was interrupted by the birth of my sister. As my caretaker held me in her arms, Momma got into a black car to leave for the hospital. Too young to understand, I sensed a big change and cried, fearing Momma had left for good. But she came back after several days with a baby who turned out to be a great companion and playmate, my sister Russell Anne, called *Russell*. Our binary star system had formed.

Our brother, William Homer, Junior, called *Billy*, came along four years later. I was old enough to understand Momma went to the hospital to have a baby and knew she would bring him home to live with us. I did not understand the origin of babies, but accepted the mystery in stride, much like scientists today seek to understand the complex origins of stars and planets. Billy became the pink angel, at least when he was asleep. A third star was added, and our orbits became stable to form the triple star system. It's difficult to say if he orbited his sisters or vice versa, and perhaps it doesn't matter, because we were connected.

Momma and Daddy prided themselves on treating each of us the same. All resources, such as clothes and toys in the early years and money and land in the later years, were equally divided, almost to the penny. But it was clear from very early that I could get away with more from Momma, Russell could get away with more from Daddy, and Billy could manage both. We formed a triangular alliance below awareness to maximize these parent-child connections to benefit the siblings. Although as individuals we differed in many ways, we were one, like a triplet of stars held together by family love.

Those of us fortunate to develop together with a brother and sister under loving parental guidance learn much about how to get along with others. We sometimes fought as children growing up together do. Like puppies at play, human siblings begin to learn the unwritten rules of social behavior and to gauge when "play nips" cross over to cause pain. We learned about cooperation but also when standing up for oneself was the better approach.

There is always some conflict in a family of strong-willed, stubborn people, especially as children move through adolescence, and our family was not exempt from life's ups and downs. But love was never in doubt. When we were small there were games, tea parties, pranks, and playing "fort" with each other, cousins, and friends. Over decades we celebrated holidays and birthdays with extended family and friends and enjoyed vacations at the beach and mountains. The memories of these times and places, featured in this collection, are consistent among the three of us. This is remarkable because siblings share a similar, but not identical, environment and recollections evolve over time.

Billy, Russell, and I were united in caring for our parents in the final years, each assuming a different role in our system. Russell lived next door to Momma and Daddy and was always on call; she also handled medication and medical bills. Billy, with accounting expertise, handled the extensive financial and estate matters; his ability to negotiate paperwork surpassed Momma's. After Momma was gone, he drove Daddy around looking at the family properties and surrounding areas. They talked about the past and history of the land and people, which meant a lot to both.

I lived further away and spent chunks of time with Momma and with Daddy on weekends and more often toward the end of each parent's life. I often interacted directly with the staff at the institutions that cared for our parents. We all took turns going to The Oaks to visit Momma. The three of us communicated continuously through group text messages and emails and met in person. Other family members helped as well. In the end, we did what needed to be done, just as Momma and Daddy taught us through example, each of us shining and dipping when needed.

These were difficult times, but we never wavered in our commitment to provide the best possible care for Momma and Daddy. We made sure someone familiar visited every day while they were in care homes. We negotiated the challenging process of providing care for ten years and ultimately divided resources without discord, working together so that strong differences of opinion never arose. The strong bond of love translated to positive action. Momma and Daddy must have done a good job raising us.

Russell and Billy provided memory assists as I wrote and feedback on the written narratives. I cannot imagine this compilation coming together without their involvement. They are the silent co-authors of the collection, orbiting and providing support and aid. Although their presence may not be evident to the reader they are always there, as in a multiple star system.

The happenstance of birth brought us together; the influences of love, shared experience, and cooperative effort connect us through good and difficult times. Even if we were not related, my sister and brother are people I would be honored to count among my most trusted friends.

VI

Family Recipes

Scoop black dirt from the edge of the soybean field and place into a large mixing bowl. Gradually add water until dirt is just moistened. Mix in one or two eggs taken from the henhouse when Momma is not looking. Beat mixture, adding small amounts of dirt, until it has a thick and frothy texture. Pour into a pie pan.

— Ruthie's Mud Pie

Each recipe in this collection was named in a story and is filled with warm memories from my childhood. These "traditional" recipes are still used in our family and are part of our own "never-ending." Sharing them with you is a way of bringing specific reminisces to life with the hope that you can create new and enduring family memories. Enjoy!

Breakfasts

Daddy's Cheese Omelets

3 large eggs
1 tablespoon margarine
About 1/4 to 1/2 cup grated cheddar cheese
Salt and pepper to taste

Break eggs into a bowl; add salt and pepper.
Whip eggs with a fork until fluffy; stir in grated cheddar cheese.

Preheat an 8- or 9-inch nonstick omelet pan over medium heat; put margarine in pan and tilt pan to coat.

Carefully pour egg mixture into pan; cook until eggs are set; fold omelet over and cook until done, and cheese is melted.

Serve immediately.

Momma's Waffles

1 cup of self-rising flour
3/4 cup whole milk
1 egg
2 tablespoons vegetable oil

Mix all ingredients into a bowl. Bake in a preheated waffle iron according to manufacturer's instructions. Yield 2 small or 1 large waffle, depending on size of waffle iron. Serve hot with syrup and sour cream.

Cinnamon Toast

Bread (Momma used white)
Margarine
Cinnamon-sugar mixture

Spread margarine on bread and sprinkle generously with cinnamon sugar.

Toast in a toaster oven until brown and bubbly.

Serve immediately.

Main Courses

Lessie's Chicken Pot Pie

<u>For Filling</u>
Whole chicken
About 2-3 tablespoons flour or cornstarch
Chopped carrots, celery and other vegetables, if desired (about 1 cup veggies to
3 cups broth)
Salt and Pepper to taste (don't over salt)

<u>For Biscuits</u>
1 cup shortening
2 cups self-rising flour
Whole milk as need for texture

Stew chicken by boiling it in water seasoned with salt and pepper. After chicken cools, pull the meat from the bones.

Make gravy with the broth by adding flour or cornstarch to one cup of broth and stirring until smooth; add flour mixture to remaining broth and stir. If broth is not thick enough, add more flour or cornstarch. Add carrots, celery and/or other vegetables to the pot pie, if desired.

Make biscuits. Blend 2 cups of self-rising flour into about 1 cup of shortening, adding whole milk to get the correct texture. Sprinkle in more flour if dough is too sticky.

Roll and cut biscuits. Lessie always cut her biscuits with a small glass.

Cover the pot pie with a layer of biscuits on top, then bake it until the biscuits are browned.

Lessie's Chicken Pilau

Whole chicken
Long or Medium Grain Rice (One cup rice to two cups broth)
Salt and pepper to taste

Boil a chicken (or hen) in water, pull meat from bones and reserve broth.

Cook rice according to recipe on bag except using broth from boiled chicken instead of water until halfway done, add chicken meat, cook until liquid is gone. Cover. Cut heat off and let sit.

Add salt and pepper to taste.

Tulls' Chicken Pilau

Tulls' Chicken Pilau included, celery, chopped up boiled eggs, and carrots.

Snacks

Daddy's Potato Chips

Baking potatoes, peeled
Deep-fat vegetable oil for frying
Salt to taste

Thinly slice peeled potatoes using a potato peeler. Place them one-by-one into deep-fat hot oil to keep them from sticking together and to avoid cooling the oil to avoid soggy chips. (Daddy sometimes got impatient and added several at a time.) Salt them generously as they came out of the oil.

Relishes

Lessie's Pepper Relish

12 finely chopped sweet red peppers
12 finely chopped sweet green peppers
1 finely chopped hot pepper
6 finely chopped medium onions
2 cups sugar
1 tablespoon salt
1 tablespoon Mixed Spices
2 cups vinegar

Cover vegetables with boiling water. Let stand 5 minutes and drain.

Cover again with boiling water. Let stand 10 minutes and drain.

Add sugar, salt, and spices (spices tied in a bag) to vinegar and simmer 15 minutes.

Add vegetables, simmer 10 minutes. Bring to a boil and pour in sterilized jars and seal at once

Lessie's End of Garden Pickle

1 cup sliced cucumber
1 cup chopped sweet pepper
1 cup chopped cabbage

1 cup sliced onion
1 cup chopped green tomatoes
1 cup chopped carrots, cooked tender
1 tablespoon mustard seed
1 tablespoon celery seed
2 cups vinegar
2 cups sugar
2 tablespoon turmeric

Soak vegetables in 2 quarts of water and ½ cup of salt overnight. Drain.

Add to vinegar and spices. Add carrots.

Boil 10 minutes.

Pour in sterilized jars and seal at once.

Canning

Lessie's Grape Jelly

<u>Supplies needed</u>:
6- or 8-quart stockpot
ladle
large spoon
strainer or cheese cloth
9 pint jars, lids, and seals (might not use them all) measuring cup, wax (optional
- Lessie used it)

<u>Ingredients</u>:
3 pounds (or more) of ripe grapes (Lessie used Muscadine)
1/2 cups of water
1/2 teaspoon butter (to reduce foaming)
7 cups sugar (do not use artificial sweeteners or less sugar)
1 pouch Certo

Rinse grapes and remove stems.
Crush grapes in stockpot.
Add 1/2 cup water.
Bring to a boil and simmer for about 5 minutes - let sit until cool enough to handle. Strain cooked grapes using cheesecloth or a strainer fine enough to prevent pulp from getting into juice (a little won't hurt). I sit a strainer on top of a bowl - Lessie used cheesecloth and tied on something and let it drip. You will need 4 cups (1 quart) of grape juice.

Pour prepared grape juice into stockpot along with:

7 cups sugar

1/2 teaspoon butter

Bring to a full rolling boil and boil (a boil that doesn't stop bubbling when stirred) Boil exactly 1 minute - stirring constantly.

Remove from heat.

Ladle into prepared jars - filling within 1/4 inch from the top. Cover with two-piece lids.

Lessie put melted wax on top of the jelly – but you can just put on the lids and let the jelly cool - the lids seal and the jelly is good for a long time on the shelf.

Be careful not to get burned when handling hot materials!

Lessie's Fig Preserves

2 quarts of figs*

1 quart of sugar*

Lemon slices

Whole cloves

Place figs (do not remove stems, do not puncture figs) in large kettle; spread sugar, 4 slices of lemon and a few cloves on top of figs. Repeat layers but be sure to leave enough room for boiling. Let stand overnight.

Next day, bring to a boil, then reduce to a simmer and continue until figs are a dark brown and liquid is a thin syrup (about 1 hour).

Seal in sterilized jars immediately with syrup covering the figs,

* or one part sugar to two parts figs for smaller amounts

Desserts

Momma's Giant Green Birthday Cake

Cake
Two boxes of yellow or white cake mix*
<u>Frosting</u>
2 sticks of margarine, room temperature
1 1-lb. box of powdered sugar
1 teaspoon vanilla flavoring
Small amount of milk as needed for spreading texture
Green food coloring

<u>Decorations</u>
1 package of premade birthday decorations
Candles

Mix cake according to package instructions; bake at 350° F in a greased and floured 10.5 x 15-inch sheet pan for about 42 minutes or until a toothpick inserted in center comes out clean. Cool 10 minutes and remove from pan (can be left and served in pan, if desired). Cool completely before icing.

For icing, combine margarine, sugar, and vanilla, mixing until well blended; add small amounts of milk as needed. Add small amount of green food coloring and mix thoroughly.

Ice with frosting and place decorations with desired number of candles on cake.
*For a smaller cake, use one box of cake mix and bake in a 9 x 13-inch pan.

Lessie's Coconut Cake

<u>Golden Glow Cake</u>
3 cups Swan's Down flour
3 teaspoons baking powder
1/2 teaspoon salt
1 cup butter
4 eggs (unbeaten)
1 teaspoon vanilla flavoring
1 cup milk

Sift flour, baking powder, and salt.

In a separate bowl, cream the butter, the add sugar (2 tablespoons) at a time, mixing well after each.

Add eggs one at a time, beating well after each.

Add vanilla flavoring, mix well.

Add flour alternately with milk - mix well.

Pour into 3 (9 inch) round pans (grease and flour pans) at 350 degrees for 30 - 35 minutes.

<u>Icing</u>
Whites from 3 eggs
2 1/4 cups granulated sugar
1/8 teaspoon salt
1/2 cup water
1 tablespoon white syrup (such as Karo)
1 1/2 teaspoons vanilla

Beat the egg whites until fluffy.

Put water, sugar, syrup, salt in a saucepan and bring to a boil, boil until the soft ball stage is reached. Remove from heat and pour into egg whites, mixing constantly. Add vanilla while mixing. Allow to cool some before icing cake.

Coconut
1-14 ounce package of Angel Flake Sweetened Coconut (will not need all of it).

Gently press the shredded coconut to cover the tops of layers and outside of the iced cake.

Tulls' Raisin Nut Cake

Soak raisins overnight
1 lb. butter and 1 tablespoon Crisco
8 eggs
2 cups sugar
4 cups plain flour
1 teaspoon vanilla flavoring
1 box white raisins (soak raisins in wine--put raisins in shallow bowl and cover with wine and let soak overnight)***
2 cups or more of cups of cut-up pecans

Blend butter/ Crisco and sugar together.

Add eggs one at a time and beat well.

Add flour 1/2 cup at a time.

Add vanilla flavoring.

When this is well mixed, add pecans and raisins.

Bake at 325 Degrees for 2 hours - test to see if done/ bake longer if not.

Saunders Family Recipe for Homemade Ice Cream

Few memories are more delicious than those of home-churned ice cream in the summertime. Here is the Saunders family recipe as recalled from my childhood.

Ingredients

3 packages of vanilla Junket Ice Cream Mix
3 anxiously awaiting children
1 pint partially whipped cream (can use ½ pint)
Momma's taste for sweetness
1 quart whole milk
1 can of evaporated milk plus 1/3 can of water (to rinse)
Daddy's attention to procedure
Sugar to taste

Optional: add fruit such as crushed pineapple, mashed bananas, slightly sweetened sliced strawberries OR fresh sliced peaches.

Equipment

Ice cream churn with electric motor
Electric mixer
Crushed ice
Rock salt
Large bowls and spoons

Step 1: Combining the ingredients

Momma mixed the ingredients from the *Ice Cream Ingredient List* in a large bowl, adding the selected fruit last. The flavors I liked best were pineapple, fresh peach, and banana. Momma and Daddy always tasted the mixture after the main ingredients were combined and debated whether sugar should be added. Momma always prevailed in this discussion and added sugar to sweeten *just a bit*. She put the cylinder fitted with a dasher into the churn, poured in the sweet mixture, and covered it with the lid.

Step 2: Churning

Daddy packed the churn with crushed ice and the proper amount of rock salt without getting any salt into the cylinder that contained the mixture. He attached the electric motor and plugged it in. The machine came to life with a crunching groan as the cylinder and dasher began turning.

Daddy timed the churning process and, most importantly, listened to the sound of the motor to know when the ice cream had reached the *Goldilocks Zone*: not too thin or too thick but just right. When it had reached the proper consistency, the motor began to struggle. This timing was important because the edges would freeze in the cylinder when the churning stopped. This made it impossible to start again if the ice cream was too soft; but if it was too firm you could damage the motor.

Step 3: Removing the dasher

When the ice cream was declared ready, the dasher had to be removed or it would freeze in place. Daddy carefully removed the dasher while scraping the frozen concoction back into the cylinder. Even after "careful" scraping, some of the frozen treat always remained on the dasher, which I now realize was deliberate. Daddy placed the dasher in a bowl that Momma had retrieved. Eager children then fell upon the dasher wielding spoons, behaving somewhat like sharks in a feeding frenzy, though sharks don't use utensils.

Step 4: Curing the ice cream

While eager youngsters were extracting every molecule of ice cream from the dasher, Daddy put the lid back on the top of the churn with a paper towel plug twisted into the hole in the top. He would drain the melted water from the churn and pack it down with more ice and salt to "cure" the ice cream for a couple of hours until time to serve it.

Step 5: Enjoying the ice cream

That amount of waiting would have been unbearable, except that we had just enjoyed the best part. The ice cream from the dasher was always a bit sweeter and creamier than the final product. In my mind, it was the main event.

I seldom churn homemade ice cream now. But when I do, I follow the traditional family recipe. It can't compare to the "main event" of earlier times, but it is sweeter with the addition of childhood memories.

Acknowledgements

Themis collection would not have been possible without support and assistance from my sister and brother, Russell Anne Potts and Billy Saunders. Thank you for your help in accessing memories and, more importantly, for your roles in co-creating our delightful childhood. I am grateful for the guidance, encouragement, review and editing from Lauren Clark on the manuscript and for the support, feedback and coaching from Dylan Critchfield-Sales on the collages; your steadfast efforts resulted in a better product and it has been a joy to work with you both. Likewise, I am indebted to Gordon Humphries for his photography which enhanced the quality of the artwork presentation. I appreciate the early support from the Primetime Writers Group and the critical eye, feedback and encouragement from the Columbia II Writers Workshop on early drafts of the stories and essays in this collection. I live in gratitude to Bud Gore and Paul Van Wyke for conversations that enabled me to rediscover radiance in life. Words are insufficient to express gratefulness to my husband, Brent Hutto for the joy of our time together in love and light; thank you for being who you are and letting me be who I am.

This collection came with the pleasure of constructing the illustrations that accompany the stories and essays. Each paper collage was assembled as part of my memory-recall and story-telling process. In some instances, the image that became a collage preceded and guided the writing process. Some were fashioned with the aid of old photographs, but many of the pictures are fanciful depictions of images from the past as I remember it. Human memory is fallible, and my writing necessarily focuses on the memories I have kept and sculpted over time. Within these limitations, I aim to stay true to my authentic self and experiences.

 This project was funded in part by the South Carolina Arts Commission which receives support from the National Endowment for the Arts.

About the Author

R uth P. Saunders retired from higher education in 2015 after 30 years of teaching, research, and service. Retirement afforded her time for her artistic side, and she began painting, drawing, and writing creative nonfiction in earnest after dabbling for years. Her first creative nonfiction book, *Lowcountry Born*, combines her passion for writing and visual arts. Ruth P. Saunders lives in Columbia, South Carolina, with her husband. Visit https://ruthpsaunders.com/

Made in the USA
Columbia, SC
22 March 2022

57760077R00122